What People Are Saying About
Let's Raise Nonprofit Millions Together

"A treasure trove of wisdom ⋯⋯⋯ ⋯g your nonprofit beyond surviving to t

Terry Axelrod
Founder & CEO
Benevon

"Karen Eber Davis's latest book tackles a huge challenge faced by virtually anyone, in any industry, who's trying to learn how to do a better job in their chosen field, and that's the challenge of translating theory into practice. We've come to expect Davis's work to be practical, straightforward, and easy to understand. She certainly delivers on that front in *Let's Raise Nonprofit Millions Together*. But this time she goes even further by setting up the bigger issues that often hamper fundraising performance but are not often addressed: the context within which fundraising happens. It gives meaning to the axiom "fundraising is everybody's business." We've all been saying that for years, but finally someone shows us what it means in practical terms."

Ellen Bristol
President
Bristol Strategy Group
Author, *Fundraising the SMART Way*

"The nonprofit playbook has become outdated. Karen takes the lead in updating our thinking; it is long overdue."

Glen Casel
President/CEO
Embrace Families

"*Let's Raise Nonprofit Millions Together* is an insightful new guide. It can benefit any organization committed to building a culture of philanthropy for game-changing growth and success. Not only does Karen simplify and demystify fundraising, but she also provides thought-provoking questions and tactics that you and your leadership team can immediately apply. Read this book and keep it handy!"

Pamela S. Harper
Founding Partner & CEO, Business Advancement Inc.
Author, *Preventing Strategic Gridlock®*
Host, *Growth Igniters Radio with Pam Harper & Scott Harper®*

"Wow! *Let's Raise Nonprofit Millions Together* should be mandatory reading for every CEO out there! Packed with information and guidance."

Hope Gwilyams
Author, *Into The Arms of Mary*

"Are you ready to raise more funds and engage more donors? *Let's Raise Nonprofit Millions Together* offers you, your board, development staff, and volunteers strategies, tools, and insider tips. Karen's insights and methods will help you to attract new donors, engage loyal donors, and build a culture of philanthropy. Chock full of excellent examples, practical and profitable tips, Karen will show you how to get everyone involved to fill your events with the right people—people who can be generous before, during, and after your benefit events. *Let's Raise Nonprofit Millions Together* is a wonderful resource for every nonprofit, NGO, school, and charity."

Kathy Kingston
President, The Kingston Auction Company
Author, *A Higher Bid: How to Transform Special Fundraising Events with Strategic Benefit Auction*

"Karen has a vast network of seasoned nonprofit executives who provide input to her work and help her bring the most up-to-date information to the marketplace, ultimately guiding organizations to raise more money, build infrastructure, and accomplish their mission goals.

From raising money to board recruitment, from staffing to strategic planning, Karen Eber Davis thoroughly researches timely topics related to fundraising and nonprofit management. She shares what she learns through her blog, videos, consulting work, and now her book."

Vicki Pugh
Vice President for Development
Palm Beach Atlantic University

"Plenty of people talk about the importance of a culture of philanthropy, but no one has compiled as comprehensive a guide to actually making it happen as Karen has. Inside you'll find specific, actionable steps for empowering your most important asset—your people—toward achieving sustainable funding."

Steven Shattuck
Chief Engagement Officer
Bloomerang

LET'S RAISE
NONPROFIT
MILLIONS
TOGETHER

BUILD YOUR CULTURE OF PHILANTHROPY

LET'S RAISE
NONPROFIT
MILLIONS
TOGETHER

HOW TO CREATE REVENUE HEROES
AT YOUR ORGANIZATION

KAREN EBER DAVIS

STILL WATERS PRESS

ISBN Print Book: 978-0-9791821-5-0

ISBN eBook: 978-09791821-6-7

Library of Congress Control Number:

13 12 11 10 9 8 7 6 5 4 3 2 1

Printed in the United States of America

ABOUT THE AUTHOR

Karen Eber Davis helps nonprofit leaders become revenue heroes. People hire Karen to help increase their revenues by up to 300 percent — what they gain are strategies that improve their organizations forever. As the award-winning thought-leader, advisor, and founding principal of Karen Eber Davis Consulting, Karen helps organizations discover propulsion tools to grow their mission, community, and revenue. Davis is known for her innovation and practicality. Besides this book, she is the author of *7 Nonprofit Income Streams*.

Join Karen's Community

Connect with Karen and her community. Sign up to receive her free newsletters and videos. Both are chock-full of insider secrets. You'll be kept up to date with complimentary educational materials including videos, articles, event notifications, podcasts, tips, and more. Learn more about Karen's community and get your supplemental materials to this book here: *kedconsult.com/LetsRaiseMillions*

Password: together

*To Frank and Preston, amazing friends, children, and human beings.
Thank you for being the best. I am one blessed mom.*

AUTHOR'S ACKNOWLEDGEMENTS

Thank you to all of the nonprofit executives, staff, board members, consultants, and friends who helped me to write this book. I appreciate your wisdom, insights, and stories, especially Craig Badinger, The Hermitage Artist Retreat; Hannah Baumgartner, Dance Now Miami; Barbara Inman Beck, Habitat for Humanity of Florida; RozeLyn Beck, Commemorative Air Force; Katrina Bellemare, Parenting Matters; Diane Bergner, Kravis Center; JL Bielon, Lions Eye Institute for Transplant & Research; Matthew S. Bisset, Eckerd College; Anne Bouhebent, Early Learning Coalition of Florida's Heartland, Inc.; Gail Bower, Bower & Co Consulting; Laura Bruney, Miami Art and Business Council; John Collins, St. Petersburg Arts Alliance; Eileen Coogan, Allegany Franciscan Ministries; Duggan Cooley, Pinellas Community Foundation; Jennifer Darling, Children's Hospital Colorado Foundation; Ethan Frizell, The Salvation Army; Janet Ginn, The Pines Foundation; Tracey Galloway, Community Cooperative; Claudia Harden, Cat Depot; Rebecca Higgins, Easter Seals Massachusetts; Kameron Hodgens, Glasser/Schoenbaum Human Services Center; Kathy Kingston, The Kingston Auction Company; John L. Lehr, Parkinson's Foundation; Kristen Lessig-Schenerlein; Jason Lippman, The Coalition of Behavioral Health Agencies; Ann Logan, Marie Selby Botanical Gardens; Mike Mansfield, Charlotte County Habitat for Humanity; Thomas Mantz, Feeding Tampa Bay; Tom McAlvanah, InterAgency Council of Developmental Disabilities; Judith Mitchell, Kravis Center; Emily McCann, Citizen Schools; Vicki Pugh, Palm Beach Atlantic University; Marina Pavlov, Florida Association of Nonprofits; Kelley Parris, Children's Board of Hillsborough County; Susan Ventura, Easterseals Florida; Jill Vialet,

Playworks; Jennifer Vigne, Education Foundation of Sarasota County; David Quilleon, Best Buddies International; Tracy Roloff, LLC; Allison Sesso, Human Services Council of New York; Sharon Stapel, Nonprofit New York; Olivia Thomas; Judy Vrendenburgh, Girls Inc.; Lora Wey, Ringling College of Art and Design; and others whom I forgot. Thank you for opening your doors and pondering with me the genius of the nonprofit world.

I am even more grateful for the friends and colleagues who helped me to weave these insights, stories, and collective wisdom into words. Thank you to my early readers: Gail Fowler, John Collins, and Becca Garcia. Your help made all the difference!

CONTENTS

FOREWORD

Armed with a fresh cup of steaming coffee, I stumble out of our rented home in Taos, New Mexico, into the chilly morning air. You wouldn't think that being in the desert in August would require long sleeves, but the high altitude causes the night air to cool considerably.

I sit down at the outdoor table and chairs and feel the cold steel against my legs and back. My fingertips are delighted to be holding warm porcelain, and the steam rises, then mixes chaotically with the pink desert sky. I watch the sun rise above the berm behind our house, an off-the-grid Earthship built of rammed earth as if emerging from the desert floor, and feel the air temperature slowly rise with it.

Suddenly, I'm aware of a humming sound. Actually, it's buzzing. It becomes louder and louder, riveting my attention. I realize it's coming from a waist-high, scrubby bush I'd barely noticed when we arrived the night before.

In the daylight, this desert plant is a tangle of spiny branches, covered with small green leaves. In the cool morning air I see that at the ends of most branches are white dots and pink fluff. Once the sun works its magic, the white dots unfurl, becoming flowers.

As the sun heats up the desert floor, an ecosystem springs to life. Honey bees swarm our little pink-fluff shrubbery, and the lizards climb to higher ground, while elsewhere in the desert the jackrabbits and coyotes nestle in for sleep.

I am merely one being, one visitor to an ecosystem, and listening to the buzzing of the bees helps flip my consciousness out of urban-dweller mode to the rhythms and patterns of the desert.

In the book you hold in your hands, Karen Eber Davis's voice is the buzz awakening you to your ecosystem. Tune in. Pay attention. And follow her advice.

Every organization—large and small—struggles somewhere along the line, and often repeatedly, with revenue generation and growth. As I tell my nonprofit clients about sponsorship development, much is out of your control, but much more than you realize is within your power.

Your organization has its own ecosystem. Karen shows you that when you activate the right elements, it too springs to life, just like our little pink fluffy shrub.

But make no mistake: Karen's ideas are not fluff. Her recommendations and methodology are strategic and nuanced, revealing the art and science of generating revenue, working with three Ps in your ecosystem:

1. people
2. purpose
3. passion

Karen teaches you how to create a culture where everyone participates in making money. All efforts count. The network of *people* to which your staff, board, volunteers, donors, clients, funders, and sponsors are connected is infinite. Flip that switch. Draw them to your organization. Watch the energy awaken and spring to life, inviting a community to swarm to you.

Karen offers a slate of skills so natural and fundamental that we humans need very little coaxing about them. She shares with us, for example, that just by being thoughtful, welcoming individuals, each member of your team can make a big difference, day after day, to other individuals who want to be part of what you're doing.

That leads us to the second asset in your ecosystem, *purpose* (or mission). In our culture today, everyone is talking about purpose. From the brands we buy to the companies we work for, we want more purpose, please. Nonprofits have missions, and the right people will be drawn to yours. People want to make a difference—in their days, years, and lifetimes. When you give people the gift of your purpose, you allow them to make a difference and contribute.

Finally, when you add the third asset, *passion*, you become irresistible. Who can say "no" to someone filled with enthusiasm about a purpose? This is your sun, the heat that causes your potential to unfurl and flower.

Your organization has life-changing value to offer your community. Karen's practical advice and great case studies will rev up all the elements of your ecosystem efficiently and creatively. Karen makes fundraising so easy and natural that *Let's Raise Nonprofit Millions Together* will become a resource to which you, your staff, and your board will refer frequently.

It's almost as good as having Karen by your side, guiding you over the finish line and bringing your vision to life.

Gail S. Bower
Revenue Strategist and Advisor
President, Bower & Co. Consulting LLC

INTRODUCTION

I've been on a quest my whole professional life to discover what works in successful nonprofit organizations. It's not an exaggeration to say that over the years I've worked with and visited six hundred nonprofits. During and after each visit, I conducted some analysis. Everything from how the signage works to what's effective, and especially what they are doing that's *brilliant*.

Over the years, I've compared nonprofits to find commonalities. I've discovered universal success patterns, excellence, repeatable processes, and how nonprofits excel despite the odds.

What you're about to read are the answers I found. They show you how to solve your nonprofit income challenge. Up until now, there have been no maps for this long-sought place. No one else has identified the strategies that make nonprofits succeed. Furthermore, no one has worked out so much about implementation.

You're about to discover a treasure chest of big-picture concepts, mindsets, and meaty tactics to ponder. Plus, you'll learn a trove of strategies. You'll refer to this book over and over again to implement the knowledge it contains.

What is the secret of successful nonprofit organizations? In a nutshell, it's this: you have incredible value to share. Because of the extent and life-changing potential of your work, everyone associated with your organization has a role to play in bringing these benefits to others.

ORGANIZATION

This book is different. Don't plan to dive in, read it in one sitting, and apply everything today. You won't find a fluffy book with a half a dozen ideas repeated for two hundred pages. After all, you need answers to tough income challenges, some that may even have plagued your organization for decades. Expect to do some thinking as you read.

You're about to meet a new friend. This friend will ask you to think and rethink about your organization and what you can do to strengthen it and make it more resilient. Like a friend with whom you meet regularly, plan to dip back into the text and topics again and again.

I divided the book into two parts. The first discusses the Let's Raise Nonprofit Millions Together approach. It tackles big nonprofit sector questions including:

1. What is sustainability?
2. How does money link with mission and community building?
3. What is a culture of philanthropy?
4. What does it mean to build relationships?
5. What do people who donated money to nonprofits value?

Part II gets specific. Here you'll read about individual roles. Boards come first because they lead. Then you'll learn how to involve your staff before you discover how to engage donors, volunteers, and customers in your efforts. You'll read about foundations, associations, elected officials, advisors, and other partners. Finally, in light of what you learn, you'll reexamine your role.

HOW TO READ AND USE THIS BOOK

1. To Understand How to Build a Thriving Organization

Read this book from front to back to construct a mental framework. Focus on the big concepts. Skim it later to use the tips and case studies to grow a thriving nonprofit.

2. For Tips to Save You Time Today

At the end of every chapter, I include time-saving tips for you to use now. For more, Chapter 11 will help you to make better decisions and master time and the gap between knowing and doing.

3. To Build a Culture of Philanthropy

Looking for a way to get everyone in your organization involved in resource development—and understanding why you need help? Focus on the contents of Chapter 3. Next, read the chapters on the supporters you wish to engage.

4. To End the Revolving-Door Development Director Challenge

The average tenure of development directors is less than three years. For practical advice on how to hire, manage, and grow successful relationships between the CEO and development staff, jump to Chapter 8.

5. To Wear It Out as a Reference

Skim the text from front to back, highlighting the parts to focus on now. Keep the book handy. You'll want to refer to it continually.

In all cases, don't forget to access additional materials at *kedconsult.com/LetsRaiseMillions*. Password: together

Karen Eber Davis
The Nonprofit Income Catalyst
President, Karen Eber Davis Consulting

THE "LET'S RAISE NONPROFIT MILLIONS TOGETHER" APPROACH

This book explores two of the three essentials of nonprofit success: money and community. This section offers guidance to help you master money and community, which will in turn create mission—the third of your success essentials.

You're already a mission expert. To up your game, you need new revenue and more fans. This book explores how to build a nonprofit that attracts both. The first half of the book explores Let's Raise Nonprofit Millions Together methods and helps you to prepare for your guests—supporters who help you to achieve your mission and who will bring you money and resources. In Part I, you'll explore sustainability, revenue streams, relationship building, and how to create more value to raise millions.

Let's Raise Nonprofit Millions Together is about transforming your people assets into revenue supporters. The results of doing this create dramatic impact. They grow revenue. Just like sports leaders who generate fan "nations," they build communities filled with fans. With each new champion, your sustainability increases.

The Let's Raise Nonprofit Millions Together approach reframes obtaining donations and income from mysterious, best left-to-experts work, to a knowable process that nurtures followers and helps them become first-class philanthropists. Using this approach, you'll realize that if only a few people at your nonprofit help to gather revenue, your nonprofit's actually acting selfishly.

CHAPTER ONE

AN INTRODUCTION TO SUSTAINABLE INCOME AND BEYOND

A nne lived in a senior facility that she moved into ten years ago. She loved books and everything about reading.

Although Anne worried about having enough resources, her attorney assured her that she had more than enough. She had enough resources, her lawyer advised, to make some significant charitable gifts.

One day at lunch, Anne and her friend Ruth discussed a recent headline about a mother's challenge finding quality childcare. Ruth shared that one friend of her family's Certified Public Accounting firm was Childrens' Services, a nonprofit that helped working parents and vulnerable children. Initially, Ruth and her husband supported the agency because their employees struggled to find quality childcare. Now that her son ran the firm, the support continued because of the exceptional work the agency did. The only problem, of course, was that the organization needed money to serve more children.

Anne called her lawyer. She asked him to research Children's Services. When her lawyer returned with a favorable report, Anne told him she had decided to make a gift. Would he start the process and notify the nonprofit?

Later that day, Anne's lawyer called the Children's Services' executive director. His client wanted to make a million-dollar gift for local children who would not otherwise receive quality care. Anne hoped her gift could, in part, be used to help children to love reading.

IS THIS JUST ANOTHER STORY ABOUT A LUCKY NONPROFIT?

Stories of unexpected gifts ripple through nonprofit headlines, boards, and gossip chains. We relish them. They give us hope. And we usually pass them off as luck.

Indeed, luck runs through this story. Anne was lucky to know Ruth. Ruth was graced with a long relationship with a quality nonprofit. Children's Services was fortunate that Anne sought an opportunity, had money to give, and cared about children. Local children were lucky to have Anne.

When we dismiss Anne's gift as a lucky break, we miss what the story illustrates about nonprofit sustainability. Nonprofit sustainability grows exponentially when you engage your supporters in gathering resources because *fundraising is for everyone*. Since conversations like the one between Anne and Ruth *will* continue, you'll grow your resources more quickly and reliably by incorporating resource development into your culture.

Let's look again at Anne's story. What's missing? Many actions large and small, over the years, that created Children's Services' success, including expressions of gratitude, invitations, and information that empowered supporters. In reality, Anne's gift resulted from the work of two executive directors, fifteen development staff members, 120 childcare teachers, fifteen parents willing to have their children photographed, three marketing and communication experts, a consultant, and others who work at and volunteer with Children's Services. Besides these insiders, let's not forget the CPAs, the employees at the CPA firm who voice their needs, community leaders who support the nonprofit's work, foundations that fund their efforts, and more. You get the picture. Numerous unnamed heroes led to Anne's gift.

When you roll back time and examine Anne's decision, you see many seeds planted in the ground. Anne's decision to make a gift to Children's Services was decades in the making. It involved hundreds of people, including the nonprofit's leaders setting a strategy to raise donated dollars, treat donors as valued assets, and involve supporters in resource cultivation.

Children's Services' "luck" is more like one falling star in a night sky filled with stars. Anne's gift's full backstory exemplifies how your supporters can help you to raise the funds you need. No CEO or development staff personnel, no matter how diligent, can replace the work that your supporters can do for you. Your supporters have the reach, trust, and power to ignite the right people at the right moment, even if they have no idea, like Ruth, that they're fundraising.

THE LET'S RAISE NONPROFIT MILLIONS TOGETHER APPROACH

Here's the critical concept. *To create sustainability in your nonprofit, incorporate an all-hands-on-deck approach.* In this example, Ruth, a long-time donor, was enthused about the cause and felt confident to share it.

This is a new way of thinking about income development. It's why I can boldly invite you to raise millions together. The one-size-fits-all solution to nonprofit revenue shortfalls is more help. To implement the solution, I'll show you how to gather more people and money around your mission.

By getting more help, I don't mean that your client will start approaching wealthy donors to request donations. Rather, you'll empower your clients, customers, volunteers, staff, board, and others to help people to become your fans who want to help you. The benefits of empowering others for your nonprofit are evident: new connections and potential donors. What's in it for supporters? The opportunity to improve lives, grow skills, gain bragging rights, and the chance to make your organization's vision real.

IMPORTANT

JOBS FOR EVERYONE

Everyone has a job gathering resources, but that doesn't mean everyone asks for money.

If we fail to connect mission and resource gathering, supporters act like money just magically appears. By linking mission activities with resource development, you get more resources and transform people into heroes, and your supporters gain skills and learn how change happens.

This book explores how nonprofits become sustainable and more. It shares how you, like Children's Services, can make resource development an organization-wide effort to succeed. I will unveil how nonprofits gather supporters and how everyone benefits from the relationships they cultivate. All that and more lies in the chapters ahead.

WHAT IS SUSTAINABLE?

Let's define *sustainable*. You've heard experts toss the word around at workshops and conferences like wrapping paper at a child's birthday party. Often, speakers use the word with little precision. Since you seek to generate millions more in resources for your nonprofit, let's get clear on what "sustainable" means. How will you know you've reached it?

Many *sustainability* definitions focus on maintaining the status quo. You may find that definition satisfactory, especially if you struggle to obtain revenue now. Over time, you'll see it as unsatisfactory. Why? Passion-driven people demand better futures than the status quo.

Here's my recommended definition:

You're sustainable when your organization develops the ability to obtain enough resources to be adaptable and operating forever.

Let's explore two concepts in this definition:

1. *Adaptable* means you have enough resources at your command to respond to new opportunities and changes, such as downturns in the market, funders who change their minds, clients who stop buying services, and donors who die. Sustainability, therefore, implies stored resources you can access to plug leaky dikes and to expand efforts, such as the ability to purchase an airline ticket today to meet with a megadonor tomorrow.

2. *Operating forever* assumes that your mission will always be required. One donor asked a mental health nonprofit what the organization would do if scientists cured mental illness. Awed by the donor's vision, the CEO answered. They would help the people who now suffered to transition to health, before closing. A day may come when your mission's complete. Until then, you need cash and resources to continue.

 BEST PRACTICES

SUSTAINABILITY: THE HABITAT MODEL

Let's move from the conceptual to an example. Habitat for Humanity offers an elegant nonprofit sustainability model. While the following simplifies it, my description shows how Habitat affiliates create three types of heroes and three distinct revenue streams.

Hero Number One: Donors. Many of Habitat's donors sprout from a dedicated pool of volunteers who join their weekly builds. Volunteers provide vast in-kind labor to build homes for the working poor. They get dirty hammering and moving sod.

Hero Number Two: Homeowners. Before they buy their home, prospective owners invest five hundred hours of sweat equity with Habitat. When they become homeowners, they make monthly mortgage payments for thirty years. The more homes a Habitat affiliate builds, the more stable the nonprofit becomes from this ongoing revenue.

Hero Number Three: Customers. Many Habitat affiliates offer resale stores that capitalize on their construction connections. These shops sell donated furniture, bathroom sinks, and other repair leftovers. Some affiliates earn enough retail revenue to cover their overhead.

WHY NOT JUST SUSTAINABLE? WHY THRIVE?

You Deserve More Money: You Do Good Work

Now that I've defined sustainability, let's explore if being a sustainable organization is adequate. Sustainable means you established a vibrant, healthy organization. This book's goal is to help you grow your resources to reach your vision. That takes thriving: the next step.

These statements lead to a fundamental premise about you and your organization, and why you deserve sustainability. This is it: you do good work. You help the illiterate to read. You put paintbrushes into frail seniors' hands. You organize programs to solve pressing public problems. You do a myriad of things to make lives better.

Moreover, you often do this work under serious constraints. Too often, you operate in a chronically resource-short environment. You must decide between buying decent office supplies or helping clients.

Nonprofit work is hard. It's not for wimps. Contrary to what you've heard, it's not government or business jobs that necessitate top skills; it's the nonprofit sector. Nonprofit leaders need the same abilities as every leader *and more.* Third-sector trailblazers, like you, work with volunteers and use skills and finesse to ask for donations. What's more, despite the challenges inherent in the work, the culture as a whole frequently looks down on the sector. The culture assumes nonprofits lacks the brightest and best.

They are wrong.

Nonprofits gather brave, smart, and ambitious people who seek to improve the communities where we live. Nonprofits collect heroes.

This includes you. Since you do good work and you provide value, you deserve money and resources. In fact, you deserve *more* money so you can generate more impact.

You chose a noble calling.

The calling requires a noble heart that appeals to the best in people and, for those who respond, the chance to become heroes. However, while you deserve more money, and it would be *fair* for you to have it, you're not entitled to it. Your noble calling doesn't require you to:

- Beg people to give to you
- Sell your clients as pitiful human beings
- Whine about your neediness
- Build your sustainability on the backs of employees
- Assume you're entitled to a gift, grant, or donation

Instead, to be sustainable, you:

- Refuse to wait for luck
- Decide to be shrewd and smart
- Study excellence
- Develop a sustainability strategy
- Use innovative twists in your work
- Embrace flexibility

I started this section with the premise that you do good work. Let's augment this principle with a second: you have reason for hope. Sustainability may feel like a big, hairy goal, and the concept of thriving a leap into the incredible. Nonetheless, grasp hope. Believe that yes, your organization can survive and thrive. Next, I share why this belief is realistic, not "pie in the sky" thinking.

 ## BRING IT HOME

YOU DO GOOD WORK AND BEYOND

To create a frame of reference for your use throughout this book, take a moment to answer these questions.

1. What exactly *is* the good work you do? How do you change lives?

2. What services or products that you provide now would be even better with more resources?

3. When, if ever, does your organization act like "doing good work" is enough and that you shouldn't be burdened with the challenge of finding resources too?

4. Do you believe that funds are short or abundant for your cause? What proof do you have for your answer?

CAN *YOUR* ORGANIZATION THRIVE?

Is it possible that your organization can thrive? Yes. Why am I, who probably never met you or examined your organization's finances, so quick to make this proclamation? My proof rests on the following fundamentals.

1. You Can Thrive Because There Are Abundant Resources

Nonprofit leaders often complain that they have too few opportunities to grow income. In reality, the challenge you face involves *too many* options. Let me lend you my binoculars so you can see the abundance.

The United States and Canadian nonprofit sectors often forgets that they operate within big economies. The United States remains the world's biggest economy; Canada the tenth.

I recently attended a presentation about three new sports enterprises near my home. I learned that guests at these venues spend millions of dollars to attend equestrian tournaments, rowing championships, and spring baseball. Did you know that on average, people spend $75 per person to attend a baseball game? You might think that $75 is not so much, so why should you be impressed? Why use this to prove abundance? Multiply this average cost by 7,400, the typical number of attendees per game, and again by the dozens of games held, and you'll perceive my point.

2. You Can Thrive Because You Bring Solutions

When you seek money for your cause, do you see yourself as:

- A child climbing on Santa's lap, promising to be good
- Avoided by donors because they don't want to be asked *again*
- A beggar who gets to dress nice

Or as someone:

- Offering an outstanding investment
- Solving tough challenges
- Remiss if you fail to share your opportunities
- Bearing good news

You, as a nonprofit leader, deliver solutions to our most difficult challenges. You improve lives. Your work offers solutions, hope, and a reason for optimism in a world of gloomy headlines, sad news, and deep conflicts.

3. You Thrive Because Others Thrive

You think of them as competition. You worry that your donors will leave you and join their ranks. You complain about their advantages. About whom do I refer? Your successful nonprofit competitors. Despite your feelings about other wickedly successful entities, their existence proves it can be done. Thriving nonprofits are success models, inspiration, and, with study, can guide you to the best paths ahead.

Why? Thriving nonprofits tap universal success patterns. These nonprofits struggle until they discover what works, and then they build around their discoveries. To this knowledge, they add tactics unique to their organization. In sum, they combine universal success patterns with unique tactics and ride them into the nonprofit revenue stratosphere. To succeed, you will also adopt the universal and add unique-to-you tactics.

One of my consulting projects involved developing a school-to-work program for a workforce development board. My client, the CEO, learned about a program in Louisville, Kentucky, at a national conference. She hired me to find funding so she could emulate the Kentucky program. Our firm's first action was not to list potential donors, government programs, foundations, and corporate partners. Instead, I investigated the origins of the Louisville program and other efforts across the country. I sought to discover *the process* used to launch successes. My client's resulting million-dollar-plus program followed the universal patterns, which she augmented unique local twists.

You can close the gap between you and other successful nonprofits. Harvest their wisdom, add your smarts, and then bushhog your own custom path to success.

Whose Job Is Sustainability?

Reaching sustainability and beyond requires a process. The first step? Design a strategy. The second? Execute it. Next? Revise your strategy with what you learn from your actions and continue to improve your outcomes.

Whose responsibility is it to make sure this process takes place in a nonprofit? Whose job is it to lead your nonprofit to thrive? Here's the short response: everyone. Here's the detailed response: creating a sustainable organization involves a multistep dance between staff, the board, and the community. The board designs and leads the dance. The staff implements what the board designs, with the help of the community.

The rest of this chapter explores the challenges that boards face when designing sustainability strategies. It starts with questions about boards' roles.

Board positions come with responsibilities. The Center for Nonprofit Risk Management states, "A board has a legal duty of duty of care that involves ensuring that there are enough resources for the organization now and in the future." Responsible boards establish the "how", that is, a strategy to make the organization sustainable. Over time, they refine the strategy to ensure it generates adequate resources.

Once you have a strategy, who executes it? In theory, staff. Figure 1 reflects the process from strategy to implementation from top to bottom.

1. The board designs a strategy that allows the nonprofit to gain adequate resources.
2. The CEO and staff execute the strategy.
3. When the strategy needs tweaking, the CEO asks the board for additional guidance.

For instance, the board decides to focus on individual donations as a major income stream. In response, the staff advises that one useful tactic to grow donors involves developing an annual appeal. The board agrees and waits to learn the results. Staff buys a mailing list of prospective donors. To the purchased list, they add the organization's existing donors and send an annual holiday appeal letter. Early in the new year, staff reports the results and the board discusses ways to tweak the strategy. That is what happens in theory. I'll return to what really happens to make the annual appeal a success later.

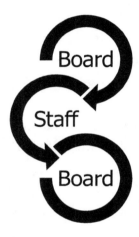

Figure 1. Whose job is sustainability?

The Conundrum

This board's responsibility to develop and fine-tune a sustainable strategy drives you straight into a dilemma. Boards must ensure nonprofits obtain sufficient resources. However, most members lack adequate knowledge about how thriving nonprofits gather income. Many work from incorrect information, e.g., they can't identify the top three sources of nonprofit income. Therefore, charging boards with creating realistic strategies is fraught with challenges.

Don't believe me? Try this. Give your board a pop quiz. In your meeting room, post the top six sources of nonprofit cash income for the nonprofit sector. They include individual donations, grants, corporate gifts, government funding, earned income related to the mission, and earned income not associated with the mission. Ask your board members to anonymously write on an index card the largest to smallest sources of income. Collect the cards. If your members are like most board members, you'll enjoy an intriguing read. (I provide more information on these revenue sources in the next chapter.)

Besides insufficient and inaccurate knowledge, boards face another challenge. Many boards, even with the best of intentions, don't know what they *don't know*. This predicament leaves CEOs in a precarious position. CEOs need to educate their bosses about nonprofit income streams, the size of different streams, and the processes successful nonprofits use to earn them, before boards can design plausible strategies.

Not in My Job Description: Should Your Board *Even* Fundraise?

Unfortunately, besides the lack-of-knowledge and don't-know-it conundrums, you face another challenge. Besides educating your board, you face a dilemma in thinking about your board's role in fundraising. One wise school of thought in the nonprofit sector advocates that boards shouldn't fundraise because boards govern. By governing well, this thinking goes, boards fulfill their duties.

Let's return to the Center for Nonprofit Risk Management's legal duty of care information. Note that the duty of care doesn't state that the board must actively fundraise or engage in revenue-seeking activities. Their responsibility is ensuring that there are adequate funds. Fundraising, of course, is different from governing. Fundraising involves helping others to express their philanthropy. Governing consists of directing the creation and administration of policy—a very different kind of work.

Here's the dilemma you face. Governing ought to be enough since quality governance can be tough and, after all, your board volunteers. Unfortunately, in the real world, nonprofits succeed by creating a large community of supporters. To thrive, you need your board's help to grow this community. You need board members to reach out and establish contacts. You need to borrow their status and prestige to promote your nonprofit into your community's nooks and crannies.

So, in theory, when your board governs well, it fulfills its responsibilities. In reality, to ensure adequate resources, board members in thriving organizations do more. To create sustainable, thriving nonprofits, boards invest their energy, reputations, and influence to grow resources. In short, the board, and everyone else, helps to raise funds.

So back, as promised, to our example board. That board, you remember, asked staff to develop an annual appeal as part of a strategy to grow donated income. Instead of waiting for the staff report after the appeal, the board got active. Several members joined an annual appeal task force. Two board members reached out to other members about a board challenge grant, and so forth. In short, the board, staff, and volunteers all worked together to create a record-breaking annual appeal to ensure the availability of adequate resources.

To help you grasp the concepts in this book, I share stories from successful nonprofit leaders in "Best Practice" sections. Your first example originates from the Early Learning Coalition of Florida's Heartland.

BEST PRACTICES

GETTING YOUR BOARD ACTIVE IN RESOURCE DEVELOPMENT

The Early Learning Coalition of Florida's Heartland's board actively gathers resources to ensure that children receive quality childcare services. Over the years, the board has engaged in helping to grow the agency's $13 million budget.

How Did They Do It?

Executive Director Anne Bouhebent shared four actions that inspired board engagement in resource development:

1. *Establishment of a Governance Policy.* Some years ago, a board member led the charge to develop a governance policy. The policy frees up the board from micromanaging and focuses their efforts on leading the organization.

2. *One-on-one Orientation.* The executive director provides an individual two-hour orientation for new members.

3. *Education.* The staff provides a fifteen-minute education session at every meeting.

4. *Meeting Disciplines.* Such as:

- Send meeting documents in advance to avoid surprises.
- Use committees to "get into the weeds" and make recommendations on individual items.
- Start and end meetings on time.
- At the appointed start time, if no quorum exists, share information items.

How Can You Adapt These Practices?

1. *Create a Governance Policy.* To help your board focus on policy, strategy, and governance, create a governance policy. Yes, you can go online to download a sample and check this off your to-do list. However, this quick-fix will cost you because, left to their inclinations, boards slide into micromanagement. Why? It requires less thinking than strategy work. To create your policy, ask your board to wrestle with the content of several different policies to create one they own.

2. *Schedule Orientations.* Conduct individual, one-to-one board orientations, so that when new members attend their first meeting, they can successfully climb on your moving train and not get run over.

3. *Education.* Busy board agendas offer little time for extras, like education. Toggle your viewpoint from seeing education as an "extra" to recognizing it as essential.

4. *Use Meeting Disciplines.* They reflect professional manners and respect for others. Well-executed disciplines reduce everyone's burdens and generate time for priorities.

Nonprofits Thrive When CEOs and Boards Decide How to Win and Everyone Helps

Obtaining adequate revenue and resources to thrive results when leaders guide an organization to create the mission and build a community that captures resources to fuel the whole operation. What's the easiest way to thrive? Assign everyone a resource-gathering role.

Once and for all, the size of the need and the complexity of creating a sustainable nonprofit settles the argument about whose job it is to obtain resources. The answer is not staff *or* the board. The answer is both and more. That is, no matter your title, you have a role to play. You can't pass the fundraising ball. The ball belongs to you. Fundraising *is* for everyone

How Will Your Organization Thrive?

Now that you know whose job it is to create a thriving nonprofit, how will your organization get there? In a nutshell: *To thrive, develop a revenue and community-building strategy that involves everyone. Apply innovative twists and consistently execute superior tactics.*

The next chapter explores the characteristics of sustainable and thriving organizations. In it, I reveal your three bottom lines and the seven nonprofit income streams you will use to fuel your work.

YOUR NOT-TO-DO TIP

NO LONG BOARD MEETINGS

At this point, I can guess what you're thinking. You're overwhelmed by the prospect of getting everyone involved in your revenue efforts. After all, you have plenty to do. You find it difficult to imagine getting everyone working on sustainability with everything else buzzing for your attention.

To help, at the end of every chapter, I'll share a task to remove from your to-do list.

Why? Thriving requires identifying what not to do *and* what to do. Here's the first tip. Construct your board meeting to fit into ninety-minute blocks of time or less. Why? You'll save time and recruit better members. Top people say *yes* more when requests come with specific obligation and time commitments.

CHAPTER TWO

HOW TO SET YOUR NAVIGATION SYSTEM TO THRIVE

I learned the importance of creating a clear vision the hard way.

On our anniversary, we dined at a restaurant called Euphemia Haye. Euphemia Haye offers two dining rooms. Upstairs is the Hayloft for quick meals and sweets. Downstairs, we submerged into candlelight and soft music. At the end of the meal, our waiter invited us up to the Hayloft for coffee and dessert.

My husband wanted coffee, so up we went. There we encountered a wall-to-wall dessert bar fit for the French diplomatic corps. Huge sugar blisters covered the apple pie. The chocolate cake included a dozen gooey layers, and the lemon pie had a meringue top the size of a football.

As I gazed at the selection, I realized my children would love this experience. "Let's bring the boys here for dessert," I said. "And let's make it a surprise for them."

When the night arrived, our surprise promise took on a life of its own. Each of our sons imagined a fantasy trip. The eldest, a fan of the book *The Hitchhiker's Guide to the Galaxy*, brought his bath towel for an intergalactic voyage. The youngest toted his Walkman and eight hours of CDs.

As we drove, we became unhappier the more we tried to explain, "It wasn't *that* big." What could have been a fun evening transformed into a colossal disappointment because of my vague destination description.

We wanted to give our children a treat. They imagined a life-changing event.

My vision of us all sharing a fabulous dessert was excellent. The vague part was the *big* mistake.

VISION FIRST

This embarrassing story illustrates several leadership truths.

The first: effective leaders lead with vision. Why? Visions motivate. People follow visionary leaders. The boys were eager for an adventure.

The second: "surprise" or vague visions don't work. Visions attract, but they need to be specific. Otherwise, you'll attract all sorts of dreams. You want people to join you to reach beautiful, new places that fit your mission, not ones they imagine.

How does vision help with raising nonprofit resources? Visions inspire those following them to invest their resources. People who believe in your vision will invest significant resources to help you to move toward a vision. Why do donors, for instance, invest millions of dollars to build a children's hospital? Because they imagine children inside the hospital getting well.

The Ordeal of Big Ideas and Vague Visions

Vision is critical because it provides fuel, orientation, and the magic that comes when the total is more than the sum of the parts, but just any vision won't do. You need a clear one. By failing to give clarity, I ruined our family's evening. However, I'm not alone. You'll find poor-clarity visions everywhere.

For example, the patriots from the Thirteen Colonies joined the American Revolution with a clear vision for liberty and self-rule. That precision led to the creation of the United States. Afterward, the new nation faced different visions, exemplified by Thomas Jefferson and John Adams's conflict about what kind of country to build.

In nonprofits, vague visions lurk behind conflicts, low morale, revenue shortage, board spats, and more. A client asked me to meet with Dorothy, a CEO, on a pro-bono basis. Dorothy was in a board struggle.

I met Dorothy in a rural part of the county in an office trailer. After small talk, she explained that she was frustrated with her board. "All they do is attend meetings."

"Tell me about your goals. What do you want your legacy to be?" I explained that I wanted to understand her goals to comprehend the board help she needed.

"To be the number-one historical destination in the state in ten years."

"Wow," I said, getting over my surprise. "So—what needs to happen to move in that direction—say to be the top local historic site in several years?"

Dorothy shrugged and repeated the goal. The more I prodded for clarity, the more she emphasized that the difficulty was her board.

Dorothy had ginned up a big, exciting idea, but not a vision. Visions stimulate imaginary pathways in your mind. Visions allow you to paint yourself into the picture. Dorothy had picked a destination that was so far away it wasn't plausible, and she had selected it alone. It was like John F. Kennedy challenging America to go to a star in a distant galaxy instead of the moon, and just picking that star all by himself.

Visions that raise millions of dollars require more than attractive concepts. Motivating visions generate fold-out maps full of routes and options. Clear visions give people a sense of where you want to go and conceivable pathways. You create them with others.

Million-dollar visions begin with bold ideas. To bring visions to life, leaders create strategies to move organizations toward the vision. These strategies attract helpers and donors who create and require plans.

What's the Difference? *Idea, Vision, Strategy & Plan*	Family Example	Nonprofit Example
Idea	Let's take the best vacation of our lives.	Men conquer prostate cancer.
Vision	Let's go out west and experience the Wild West like our ancestors.	Because of our work, men will no longer get or die from prostate cancer.
Strategy	We'll go to a dude ranch to learn to be cowboys.	To raise money and awareness, we're going to challenge men to grow mustaches in November.
Plan	We depart on the first Saturday of June at 6 a.m.	We launch our campaign on October 10.

You don't need perfect foresight to create a million-dollar vision. Instead, construct your best guess about an achievable future, so people can see how your vision will propel the organization to a wonderful new place.

Test Yourself:
Which Is It—Idea, Vision, Strategy, or Plan?

The words "idea," "vision,""strategy," and "plan" get used a lot in nonprofit organizations. They also get confused. To keep the words straight in your head, categorize the following statements: idea=i, plan=p, vision=v, and strategy=s.

1. It would be nice to end world hunger.

2. Send the annual appeal letter in November.

3. Challenge local businesses to compete for a prize based on the amount of kids' summer snacks they collect in June.

4. No child in our region suffers from malnutrition.

5. Everyone needs education in an outdoor setting.

6. This summer, I'll visit every principal on our mailing list to schedule their school's trip to our outdoor education program.

7. Every child completes an outdoor education experience day by the time they graduate from sixth grade.

8. Get the school board to include outdoor education as a mandatory part of the elementary school's curriculum.

How did you do?

The answers:

1. Idea; 2. Plan; 3. Strategy; 4. Vision;

5. Idea; 6. Plan; 7. Vision; 8. Strategy.

BEYOND VISIONS: OTHER PREREQUISITES OF SUCCESSFUL NONPROFITS

The Three Bottom Lines of Thriving Nonprofits

You've read why you start with a vision and how visions help. Visions are a first step. To create a thriving organization that raises millions, you need more.

Before you erect a building, you hire an architect so that the plumbers, electricians, and drywall installers understand your intent and coordinate their efforts. More important, you hire an architect to construct a well-functioning building. Likewise, to build a thriving organization, you need to be sure everyone understands what you're making and how to coordinate efforts.

Unlike governments and businesses that seek a single bottom line (votes and profits, respectively), nonprofits grow three bottom lines. In the next section, you will learn about them.

Question: What Are Nonprofits' Three Bottom Lines?

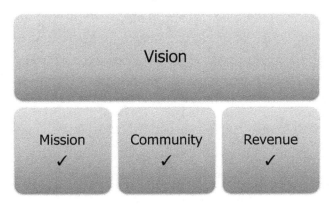

As I presented, the hall was dark except for the stage lights. The audience included nonprofit experts, CEOs, development directors, service managers, CPAs, board members, and the like. It was early in the presentation. I asked, "What are your nonprofit's bottom lines?"

A few hesitant hands rose. When I called on them, I heard mission accomplishments. "We alleviate hunger." "People newly released from jail get job training." "Dog owners bring pets to visit shut-ins." As I nodded, everyone started calling out their stupendous mission accomplishments.

Everyone was right. Your mission is your number-one bottom line.

I reminded them that the mission doesn't stand alone. "Look." I pointed out two other buildings that flank the mission on the slide. "You need these structures to succeed, too. These flanking buildings hold the fuel that gives energy to your mission work. What are they?"

In the audience, a CFO, a CPA board member, and a banker shouted out the answer: "Money." Then, someone yelled Kaiser Permanente's slogan: "No margin, no mission."

"You got it," I told them. "You must also build a flow of adequate revenue. You need money and in-kind gifts."

I shared with the CPAs, CFOs, and bankers what they already knew and what everyone else in the audience needed to remember. "To be viable, your nonprofit needs to earn money over what it costs you to operate. Moreover, even the most successful nonprofit in the world wants to see their bottom lines grow."

Heads nodded in agreement.

"I learned over the years that you have another bottom line, a third skyscraper you're building. What is it?" The audience hushed.

I gave some hints. "How many of you are 501(c)3s?" Alternatively, if I'm in Canada, I asked about registered charities: "Why did you get your special tax status?"

The answers began and soon hit the mark. "We serve the community." "People." "Volunteers." "Advocates." Spot on.

 BRING IT HOME

YOUR STRENGTHS: ARE YOU BEST AT GROWING YOUR MISSION, REVENUE, OR COMMUNITY?

Rank your organization on a one-to-ten scale, with ten representing a high score, on your success with each bottom lines.

- mission
- revenue
- community

Of the three, where do you need to do the most thinking and work?

Your third structure, or bottom line, to grow is a community. It's the final resource you need to create sustainability and to raise millions. It's the *together* in *Let's Raise Nonprofit Millions Together.* To succeed, grow a community who embraces your mission as their own.

The community you construct is your link to money and resources. Even though not everyone in the community will provide your nonprofit resources, many will. Some people will make one-time purchases and donations. Others will, with your help, participate over and over again, helping you to form a culture of philanthropy.

To rapidly move toward your vision and thrive, you need mission, money, and people. Your fastest path to your vision involves developing all three simultaneously.

 LOCATION CHECK

WHERE ARE WE? VISION, YOUR THREE BOTTOM LINES, AND MONEY

By this point, you may be asking, "What does determining a vision and recognizing your three bottom lines have to with raising millions of dollars together?"

A lot.

We began this book with the premise that you have abundant income opportunities. To take advantage of these options, you'll need help.

Imagine you're the owner of a cherry orchard full of ripe fruit. You want to maximize your yield so you can earn money to plant more orchards (your mission). Your harvest strategy involves the use of multiple crews, so you need a lot of people. First, you'll send your expert laborers—that is, your CEO, development staff, and board chair—to pick the early ripening fruit with high value. Next, you'll send your new board members and other staff to pick fruit. Finally, you'll seek the help of gleaners to find "hard-to-see" fruit hidden under branches and tucked behind leaves. They include your donors, customers, volunteers, and other partners.

Before anyone enters the field, you share your plan, organize the teams, and educate them so they recognize ripe fruit and know how everyone will benefit from the experience. You need a unifying vision, a strategy, and plans, or else everyone will head into the orchard at the same time, overpick some trees and miss others, and wander into other farmers' fields. You need the vision to remind everyone why they're sweating in the sun.

That's the role of vision and your three bottom lines in raising millions together. That's our location now. What's next? Exploring nonprofit revenue streams, so you can help others to understand what's available to your nonprofit.

The Shocking Truth: You Have Too Many Opportunities for Revenue, Not Too Few

Figure 2. The confusing world of nonprofit revenue opportunities.

We return to our unlit presentation room. On the screen, there was a slide of a pie chart with six slices and, to the side, a list of nonprofit income streams. One slice of the pie filled almost half the pie. "This pie," I explained, "illustrates how nonprofit organizations earn cash."

I asked people to stand and pair with a neighbor. I challenged each pair to decide which of the six income sources listed depicted the biggest slice of the pie.

The choices included:

- individual donations
- corporate funding
- grants and foundations
- mission revenue (selling goods and services related to your mission)
- nonmission earned income
- government

(Before you read on, take a moment to decide. What's your answer?)

Mumbles of conversation filled the room. Since the request seems straightforward, the room quieted quickly.

"Ready?" I asked. They nodded. "If you guessed government funding, please sit down." Twenty percent of the room sits. "Government funding is about a quarter slice of the pie. You made a solid guess."

I continued. "Have a seat if you guessed individual donations." Moans of disbelief ensued. Half of the room sat. "Individual donations," I shared, "represent the largest source of *donated* income. As you can see from the list, not all cash revenue is donated. Donations, which include bequests, equal about 25 percent of the sector's cash income."

We'd identified half the pie. What remained? The biggest slice and three small ones. The next guesses were grants and corporate funding.

These groups sat down. Each of the streams represented the two smallest slices. Year after year, corporate funding remains the tiniest, followed by foundations and other nongovernment grants.

Two slices remained. They make up more than half of the sector's cash revenue. A handful of people remained standing. Even in the dim light, you could see their Cheshire-cat smiles. They knew the answer, and not coincidentally: they run well-funded nonprofits.

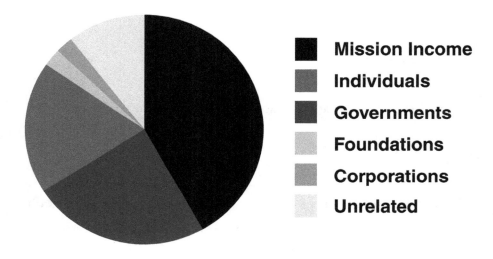

- ■ **Mission Income**
- **Individuals**
- **Governments**
- **Foundations**
- **Corporations**
- **Unrelated**

The Big Reveal

The remaining sources, which represent over half of the nonprofit sector's income, are two kinds of *earned* income. The smaller slice, about 10 percent of the sector's revenue, reflects products or services that nonprofits sell that don't have anything to do with your mission. For instance, the water and cookies you sell in your gift shop.

The big slice represents mission income. It encompasses all the products and services that nonprofits sell that provide revenue *and* support mission results. Examples include rent paid by individuals in supportive housing, museum ticket sales, and childcare tuition.

Let me sidestep here to remind you that the pie shows the sector's income. This is not a prescription, just a collective picture of how nonprofits obtain cash. My research into individual organizations matches the chart. Most nonprofit organizations obtain most of their income from the three top sources: mission revenue, government funds, and individual donations. The other sources—grants, corporate funding, and earned income unrelated to the mission—provide the rest.

FUNDRAISING FUNDAMENTAL FOR EVERYONE

In your quest to raise nonprofit millions, your supporters need basic knowledge about nonprofit revenue. Here are five critical concepts to share with your supporters.

1. How You Earn Income

Your supporters need to know how your nonprofit earns income. They'll benefit from understanding how you obtained revenue in the past and your ideal future revenue streams.

2. Why You Need More Revenue

People who care about your work need to understand why your organization needs more revenue. You want them to know why your current income streams are inadequate. Let them know how new revenue will help you to accomplish your mission and reach your vision.

3. FAQ Knowledge

A massive public misunderstanding exists about how nonprofits use resources, so your supporters need to become confident in answering questions about how you invest your resources. Help them to answer frequently asked questions such as why there are "high" salaries, why the work is expensive, and other questions that you hear about your organization's revenue.

4. Stories About How Money Arrived

Hearing stories about how the money arrived will convince your coworkers that their efforts matter. They need to hear how donors and customers got recruited, stayed involved, and found value. By sharing origin stories, you'll answer questions in your supporters' minds, such as: How did the organization and the person providing the revenue meet? How many interactions took place between the two parties before the investment was made? How long did it take?

5. The Payoff

Like donors, your helpers need to know that you notice and appreciate their efforts. They need to understand that you celebrate them stepping into new space to help the cause. They'll benefit from learning how their actions contribute. You want them to grow in awareness that they belong to a growing culture of philanthropy and that their philanthropy will create results in the cause they hold dear, the lives of those who get involved, and their own lives.

From Vision to Money

Having failed on the dessert adventure, we took our sons on a big trip to Europe. This time, we told them the overall plan and invited them to help form the itinerary. I warned them, "You'll get tired of looking at castles." They packed appropriately and promised me they would *never* tire of seeing castles.

I was right. After a while, when I shouted from the front seat of the camper van, "Look, a castle!" they didn't flinch from their Game Boys.

You, too, can predict the future. How? Your vision sheds light on it. To reach your vision, grow your mission, community, and revenue. This chapter provided an overview of nonprofit structure and revenue streams and what to share with your supporters to raise millions together. Next, you'll explore community building. Before closing, here's your next not-to-do task.

YOUR NOT-TO-DO TIP

SAY NO TO LOW-RETURN REVENUE OPPORTUNITIES

"Perfection is achieved, not when there is nothing more to add, but when there is nothing left to take away." —Antoine de Saint-Exupéry, Airman's *Odyssey.*

Stop pursuing money that provides poor returns. It's like surfing. Let the little waves pass so you have the energy to ride the big ones. After winning a $1,000 grant that required a three-page application and three staff members to participate in a check presentation banquet, a client decided to only apply for grants smaller than $2,000 if they could be obtained and managed in less than five hours of staff time.

CHAPTER THREE

DON'T TRY THIS ALONE: WHY YOU NEED TOGETHER AND WHAT IT LOOKS LIKE

"Nonprofits can become lazy in the presence of a healthy endowment," explained Dr. Kameron Hodgens, executive director of the Glasser/ Schoenbaum Human Services Center. The organization she leads houses nineteen social service nonprofits.

The center's founder, Dr. Kay Glasser, prepared for the future. Along with building the five-acre campus, she gathered an endowment to allow the center to charge below market-rate rents.

So what's wrong with a lazy nonprofit if you've covered operating expenses? To be sure, slothfulness with an endowment *is* better than slothfulness without one. Why do leaders, like Kameron, in the enviable position of routinely earning substantial revenue, still benefit from an all-hands-on-deck approach to resource growth?

When folk disengage (which happens when revenue needs disappear), results decline. The siren call of the vision gets muffled. Over time, if nothing changes, you attract visionless board members and staff. Before you know it, decay runs deep and the nonprofit dies. You can have all the money you need to survive, but unless *more* happens, you won't thrive. You won't reach your vision. You won't raise millions together.

BUILDING A THRIVING ORGANIZATION PERSON BY PERSON

People at Your Fingertips

Part of the challenge for visionary leaders like Kameron, as if the threat of decline wasn't enough, is the ready access she has to excellence. Visionary leaders know that access to a thriving nonprofit stems from two numbers.

Drum roll for the numbers, please.

They are six hundred and two hundred.

Experts estimate that everyone knows six hundred people. Other specialists, who focus on specific connections, tell us that most people have two hundred close contacts; that is, people you can invite to a wedding or, less cheerfully, a funeral.

Either number justifies involving tons of supporters in resource development. Why?

Even though nonprofits crave more money, what most organizations need is more *meaningful relationships*. By this, I mean connections with people who, with a little nurturing, become your fans. Fans bring resources, including money. They produce fresh solutions. They stir up the resolve to achieve your vision. What's more, existing supporters benefit from meeting new fans. It affirms their involvement. It inspires them to invite others. When enthusiastic fans attract more enthusiasts, you fall into an avalanche of possibilities.

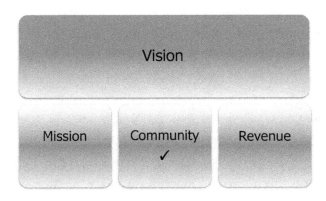

How can you meet people with fan potential? That's what the numbers six hundred and two hundred tell us. Are you ready to discover the arithmetic logic of raising millions together?

I return to my client Kameron. If she's average, she knows six hundred people. Kameron, however, runs a nonprofit, was raised in town, and is *very* personable. In all likelihood, her circle of acquaintances exceeds six hundred. However, since some of her acquaintances include her preschool daughter's friends and other "not prospects," let's assume Kameron's circle of influence equals six hundred individuals. These people include many who will take her calls and some who will accept her invitations to attend an event.

Kameron doesn't take on this challenge alone. The Glasser/ Schoenbaum Center's board has seventeen members. Each, chosen for their leadership, can identify six hundred people. (Skeptical? I just returned from a dental appointment. The office includes a dentist, the dentist's assistant, the hygienist, and the receptionist. Do I know them well enough to invite them to a nonprofit event? Yes, I do. For crying out loud, I let three of them put their hands in my mouth!) Seventeen times six hundred equals 10,200 individuals. However, to keep you from throwing this book or your reader across the floor, let's assume that each board member will only identify two hundred contacts. Seventeen times two hundred totals 3,400 individuals.

Three staff members serve the center. Again, sticking with two hundred acquaintances, the staff in total knows six hundred people. By adding Kameron's six hundred connections, her board's 3,400 friends, and the staff's six hundred acquaintances, the center has a direct relationship with 4,600 people. My point? *You* know many people.

Executive Director = 600
Staff 3 x 200 = 600
Board 17 x 200 = 3,400
_____

Total people 4,600

Now, let's consider how you can reach them. Who is the most effective person to contact these friends and acquaintances? You guessed it—the people who already know them. They're literally at your fingertips. You, your staff, and the board can reach them with a text, call, email, or meeting.

Collectively, these individuals are the easiest and best people for your organization to invite to join your efforts, and if they like what you do, to become your fans. They represent your Magic Circle of Next. Out of everyone in the world, you have the best chance of successfully inviting your direct contacts and friends.

YOUR MAGIC CIRCLE OF NEXT

Here's an alternative way to visualize your prospective fans. This time I use the concentric circles of a dartboard to illustrate it.

Notice the inner circles. They represent your CEO, staff, and founder. The next ring includes your board, followed by your donors, customers, and volunteers. Moving outward, you find foundations, associations, elected officials, advisors, and other partners with whom you conduct business. Collectively, these individuals each know two hundred people well enough to recommend your work and often to

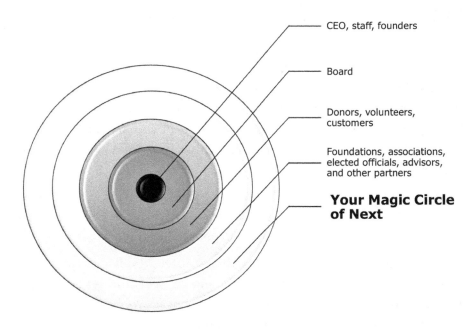

CEO, staff, founders

Board

Donors, volunteers, customers

Foundations, associations, elected officials, advisors, and other partners

Your Magic Circle of Next

share an invitation from your organization. When they do this, they reach your Magic Circle of Next.

The diagram illustrates opportunities to grow your community. Every time someone in your circle connects with someone new, your Magic Circle of Next expands. For example, you hold a discovery meeting with a potential sponsor. The prospect invites two other division managers from her firm to the meeting. After the meeting, you send follow-up thank-you notes to all three people. You just expanded your Magic Circle of Next.

If you need more people in your pipeline to become donors, volunteers, or customers, your best place to find them is in your Magic Circle of Next. Initiating these relationships will energize you. You'll notice new faces. Your pipeline will swell with potential supporters. Some of the crowd will become part of your fan nation.

LOCATION CHECK

WHERE ARE WE?

In this chapter, you learned why it's wise to grow your community, even if you have a huge endowment, and you've been introduced to your Magic Circle of Next. Meeting people, of course, is not enough. You need to connect with newcomers. Otherwise, folks will fly in and immediately fly out.

How can you increase the odds that, once you invite people, they'll stay around long enough to fall in love with you? What types of actions create the kind of culture that attracts people like a Black Friday sale?

You'll find the answer in the rest of this chapter. You'll learn about six resource development skills that will help you to capture newcomers in the Karen's Friends and Fortune Flowchart. You'll learn how to establish a process to engage newcomers to benefit everyone.

Specific Help You Need

You follow the logic. Engaging more people helps you to reach others with your message. You want as many people as possible to meet you at your best. What can you do to introduce your best self to potential enthusiasts? Karen's Friends and Fortune Flowchart outlines the specific behaviors that will help you to raise millions together.

INTRODUCING KAREN'S FRIENDS AND FORTUNE FLOWCHART

Karen's Friends and Fortune Flowchart identifies six behaviors that, when woven together, form a welcome mat that will endear your organization to newcomers. Each skill supports fundraising and resource development. Consistent use of these behaviors in your

50

nonprofit supports a community of people who want to be part of your organization and will bring resources to you.

Karen's Friends and Fortune Flowchart

	Benefits Most →		
Relationship Skills ↓	Prospect	Nonprofit	Both
Connect Build	Host	Speak	Solve
Develop	Invite	Collect	Introduce

The Organization of the List

Here's how to read the flowchart. The skills in each of the two rows of the matrix reflect relationship growth. First, people connect and build relationships. Second, they develop as philanthropists.

Reading left to right across the matrix highlights the groups that benefit the most when the skills get used. The choices include the prospective supporter, the nonprofit, or both. By pointing out who gains the most, I'm holding up my hands and waving them to get your attention. Please notice the uneven exchange of value. In any given transaction, value might be one-sided. That's okay because over time, exchanges balance out.

Inside the matrix, the six skills begin with the easiest and move toward greater difficulty. Most people find connecting less challenging than developing. For example, hosting (skill one) is easier than intentionally introducing people to others (skill six).

With those preliminaries aside, let's explore the skills. In the section below, you'll learn more about the skill, read examples, learn how each fits with fundraising, and discover what you lose when you don't use it.

LEVEL A: CONNECT AND BUILD

Research verifies the cliché that you only get one chance to make a first impression. Connecting skills help you to maximize initial contacts with prospective donors, customers, and supporters. These actions take advantage of the brief window when newcomers form first impressions. Successful use of these skills conveys welcoming, information, and enthusiasm.

Skill One: Host

What Is Hosting?

What was the last formal event you watched or attended? Perhaps, it was the Academy Awards, a wedding, or even when your friends pulled out their good china and invited you to dinner.

At these gatherings, someone acted as the host. Hosts welcome guests. They take their coats, offer drinks, and invite newcomers to join the festivities. Hosts include others during events, such as your gala, board sessions, and office visits.

Hosting involves more than just saying "hello." Hosts notice when individuals stand alone. They notice when people get excluded, ignored, and disconnected. Hosts toss them a line to belonging. Hosts observe what's needed and seek to provide it. They steer conversations and rearrange activities to engage everyone. When successful, the host connects people on the edges to the center.

Hosting provides two distinct benefits. It demonstrates how your organization treats everyone with dignity. Second, it empowers the host. When you host, you don't just support an organization. You lead it.

BEST PRACTICES

DOES HOSTING WORK?

When L. David Marquet, author of *Turn the Ship Around!*, began to lead the nuclear submarine the *Santa Fe*, the ship's rank was at an all-time low. Despite this, Marquet asked everyone to *act* as if they enjoyed the top spot.

Crewmembers were instructed to greet visitors by name, give their name, and welcome them to the *Santa Fe*. Initially, even with military discipline, only one-third of the personnel complied. However, even at this compliance rate, the submarine's ranking jumped from subpar to above average.

How Does Hosting Help Fundraising?

People have many philanthropic options. Donors remain, for good reasons, cautious beings. Before they donate, they often carefully investigate nonprofits. To vet you, some donors choose side doors. That is, they ask for help to make their donation from someone who seems unassuming—the person cleaning up, at the front door, or a volunteer. They intentionally avoid contact with the development staff, the CEO, and board members. Your community's willingness to host will convince these donors to conclude your organization is a worthwhile investment.

What Happens When We Forget to Host?

You lose resources and friends. When you act as a host, people remember you.

Skill Two: Speak

What Is Speaking with Hope and Enthusiasm?

Using this skill, the second in the flowchart, asks your supporters to express positive views about your organization when talking or writing about the nonprofit. Supporters practice this behavior in your facilities, in the community, and when they gather with friends and family. Speakers use the skill because they remember that the person with whom their connecting might be meeting your organization for the first time.

Before exploring the value of this skill, let's double back to the phrase "express a positive view." Speaking this way doesn't involve lies, exaggerations, or Pollyanna's sunshine. Rather, it communicates your vision of hope. Speaking with hope demonstrates that change can come through words.

Telling is a more advanced form of speaking. Speaking follows an external prompt: someone asks about your organization. Telling, in contrast, requires your supporter to insert minimission stories into conversations.

Why Is Speaking with Hope and Enthusiasm Important?

Speaking reflects optimism. Optimism attracts. Since people seek winning causes, not imploding efforts, you gain when your supporters express optimism.

Learned optimism contrasts with learned helplessness, which is where supporters might meander if they fail to use this skill. Learned optimism, a concept from positive psychology, demonstrates that hope, like other skills, can be cultivated. For example, telling ourselves that a donor didn't fund us because our stories aren't compelling—meaning that we lack the ability to attract donors—discourages us from telling again. In contrast, telling ourselves that a donor didn't fund us because the story we told didn't resonate with them—something we can change—encourages us to try again.

Telling mission success stories conveys the substance of your work in easy-to-remember nuggets. When you use this skill, you distribute gems of hope to others. Stories help people to connect to your work on an emotional level. Logic makes us think. Emotions make us act. Speaking calls forth new philanthropic heroes.

 BEST PRACTICES

DOES TELLING STORIES WORK?

One day, Becky Higgins, the development director at Catholic Charities, worked at home so her plumber could fix her kitchen sink.

"What do you do for a living?" the plumber asked, twisting a wrench.

After she told him, Becky handed him the organization's newsletter and said, "Look at this. It tells the story better than me. It's all good news. Look at what we do for the people here. Would you like me to send you the newsletter?"

He said, "Yes." The next month, Catholic Charities received a $250 check from the plumber, and every other month after that.

How Does this Skill Help with Fundraising?

Speaking helps others to learn about your work and gives them a reason to support it. Here's an example. Years ago, a client asked me to write a grant application for an organization that served homeless mothers. The previous grant cycle, the proposal had been rejected. From reading the earlier request, I learned that homeless mothers were in dire straits. The application, even if fully funded, would barely improve their lives. As a consultant, I rewrote the piece to share hope, casting the foundation as the hero. My client received $250,000 and, six months later, a second grant. Speaking with enthusiasm and optimism triggers delightful surprises—including more resources.

What Happens When We Forget to Speak Enthusiastically?

Without enthusiastic speech, we dampen participation. When you forget to tell stories, the valuable progress they portray gets ignored. An untold story doesn't have a chance to leave a profound impression in supporters' minds. Potential fans don't hear your good news.

BRING IT HOME

WHAT IS THE FRIENDS AND FORTUNE FLOWCHART EXPERIENCE LIKE FOR A VISITOR AT YOUR ORGANIZATION?

Imagine you've been called for a meeting with a nonprofit about potentially volunteering to support their work. As you wait in the reception area, you're impressed. By the time you meet your appointment, you've decided that no matter what happens during or after the interview, you'll donate to this group. What happened? What did you see? What did people say to you to inspire your response? List everything that generated your outstanding impression.

Now imagine you're visiting your organization. What do visitors experience? How will you close any gap?

Skill Three: Solve

What Is Solving?

Solving offers assistance to newcomers and others. It answers their challenges. Using this skill allows your organization to help others. Solving starts with learning. You begin by asking or fielding questions, such as: "Can I help you find someone?" and "Welcome to our nonprofit, how can I help you?" and "What brought you here today?"

What does solving look like? Stop by Trader Joe's. Ask a staff member for the olive oil. The clerk walks you to the aisle, positions themselves in front of the display, and gestures to your oil options.

In preparation for an online panel, Kathy Kingston, auctioneer extraordinaire, asked one of her clients for a favor. Without hearing the request, Sister Mary Alice replied, "Anything you need." Sister Mary Alice was practicing solving. Solving also includes giving a quick tour, grabbing boxes from a donor's car, calling back folks who leave messages in your general voice mailbox, and more.

Why Is Solving Critical?

Solving bumps up hosting a big step. People begin interacting with your organization with a goal. The quest may be to use your services, volunteer, or donate. They might seek to satisfy their curiosity about your mission after years of driving by your site. Offering help establishes a relationship between a newcomer and an organization insider.

Students learning improvisation discover that when they reply, "Yes, and...," dialogue builds. If they reply, "No," or "Yes, but...," the dialogue contracts. Likewise, solving seeks to say, "yes, and..." to challenges and needs. Solving engages your organization in another's journey. Solving creates a community of yes.

Finally, over time, regularly solving people's concerns helps you to discover ways to improve your processes and streamline your operations.

Does Solving Work?

While serving a nonprofit with an annual budget of $65 million, a savvy staff member received frequent telephone calls from reporters asking about the CEO's salary.

The staff member identified the need behind the question: the reporter wanted a story. In response, she solved the reporter's need by meshing what the reporter wanted and what the nonprofit needed—good press. Instead of salary data, the savvy employee offered the reporter an exclusive story. By responding to the need, not the request, she better served the reporter, the nonprofit, and the community.

How Does Solving Help Fundraising?

Offering help moves fledgling relationships into new places—where give and take can become the norm. By offering to help, you give a person a small gift: your willingness to help. You initiate the rule of reciprocity. Robert Cialdini, the author of *Influence*, explains that all cultures teach that "thou shall not take without giving in return." When you solve, you prime the pump to commence a relationship of mutual support. That is, solving begins a potential process where you exchange value, helping each other out, over and over again.

What Happens When We Forget to Solve?

When you forget to solve, you lose money, supporters, and customers. I attended a meeting where a leader made a special plea for donations. I wanted to give and had a $20 bill stuck in my calendar.

I approached two volunteers with the bill in hand. "I'd like to give this. How can I?" They didn't know. I perused the room for an envelope or a donation box. Finally, I found a frenzied staff member who accepted the money.

People don't want to work hard to help you. When you fail to solve, needs go unmet, opportunities get lost, and minimissions fail.

 BEST PRACTICES

THANK-YOU LUNCHES

"One of the things we have found to be effective are thank-you luncheons," said Judith Mitchell, CEO of the Kravis Center for the Performing Arts. "We invite donors to the center for lunch. We talk about their vacations, families, or whatever. No one makes an ask."

Staff schedule luncheons when donors complete pledges or after large annual gifts. Attendees include the donor couple, the CEO, the board chair, development staff, and sometimes other board members.

For donors, lunches offer valuable extended face-time. Afterward, one donor shared how much he enjoyed the meal and how nice it was "not to be asked for money."

According to Diane Bergner, Senior Director of Development, the payoff for the center includes high renewal rates, loyalty, and an increased chance of the donor becoming a goodwill ambassador for the center.

How Can You Adapt This Practice?

Let's explore the replicable magic behind appreciation luncheons:

First Magic: One Agenda. Lunch together. That's it. There's no other agenda, hidden or otherwise.

Second Magic: The Timing. The invitations arrive after receiving gifts. You use the lull between when it's too soon to ask for another donation and when it is time for the next request. You allow your donors to luxuriate in your institution's gratitude.

Third Magic: The Exclusivity. I heard you sigh as you read about this practice, "I don't have time for three-hour lunches." Not to worry. Make them an exclusive perk, offered to the donors you most want to connect to, so you enjoy them.

The Deep Magic: Your Gift of Time. Your presence is the most magical part of these luncheons. Your donors admire your work. Many would like to count you as a friend.

LEVEL B: DEVELOP

The set of skills in this section brings together information, people, and resources to help you form deeper relationships.

Skill Four: Invite

What Is Inviting?

Inviting runs the gamut from asking, "So will we see you at the volunteer event next week?" to requesting your friends join you at special events. Besides verbal requests, you invite with emails, newsletters, and social media. This skill connects a prospect to a next step. When used regularly, community members who enter your sphere of influence receive suggestions on what to do next.

You already offer many invitations. Using the inviting skill makes the process more intentional organization-wide. It's as if you're building a superhighway. To serve people better, you add lots of on-ramps— that is, invitations.

In most cases, inviting doesn't involve asking for money, except incidentally. Examples include encouragement to attend events with fees or participate in group fundraising events, such as marathons. When there are fees, they're not the purpose of the invitation. The aim is to move the invitee closer to the nonprofit.

Why Is Inviting Important?

You'll see I listed inviting under "helping the prospect" in the Friends and Fortune Flowchart. Are you surprised? It's here because you don't invite to fulfill your organization's needs. You invite to help people take their best next step.

Inviting succeeds when your invitee learns about and takes an action that matches their interests. Inviting, at its best, moves outsiders over time into your organization where they fit best.

Does Inviting Work?

To learn why inviting works, do a little mental multiplication. When inviting becomes an organization-wide habit, you'll drive up your event participation by 10 percent or more. For instance, if twenty individuals make one request per week and 10 percent of people who would not have otherwise attended participate, your attendance just bumped up by one hundred people. My clients typically discover that system-wide use of inviting stimulates growth of participation upward of 25 percent the first year.

What Happens When We Forget to Invite?

When you forget to invite, you reduce your impact. You forfeit the chance to share your value and for others to receive your benefits. Your invitees lose the opportunity to improve their lives. When you invite, in essence, you say, "I value you enough to make an effort to include you."

How Do Invitations Help Fundraising?

The skill solves a critical development need. That need is to build a sizable pool of individuals with a connection to and an in interest your organization. Invitations grow this pool.

BEST PRACTICES

FILLING TABLES

During a manager's meeting, Mike Mansfield, CEO of the Charlotte County Habitat for Humanity, announced, "Everyone needs to sell seats for a gala table."

The response? He saw the top of everyone's head.

Mike persisted. "You *must* be part of this organization—being part of it involves more than spending money. It involves raising it."

Despite the initial response, each of Mike's managers filled a table. What happened? Habitat benefited from a successful special event. The managers grew their invitation skills.

How Can You Adapt This Practice?

Let's look at the replicable ideas in Mike's request. I call them *magic spells.*

First Magic Spell: Provide a Long Lead Time to Help Inviters to Fill Tables. Prompt them on how to use the time well. For example, a board member might mention the event to friends, hint that he'll be asking, and even make preliminary plans with his contacts three months before your next gala.

Second Magic Spell: Build Accountability into Your Requests. Mike didn't only announce his expectations. He asked for progress reports.

Third Magic Spell: Reward People who Invite Others. Many people will perk up at the chance to gain recognition. Others enjoy competing. Some don't want to be left behind. Acknowledgments, pats on the back, and awesome work proclamations support inviters and fill event tables.

BRING IT HOME

THREE CHEERS FOR YOUR TOOLBOX: INVITING SKILLS

Here's a process to ramp up the number of invites your staff offers:

Create a Unique Email Address.

When a team member offers an invitation, ask them to report the invitation to the unique address. In the subject line, he or she writes the offer. In the body of the email, the inviter notes the person or people invited.

Send an Automated Response.

Include a thank-you note, cute quote, or another electronic pat on the back.

Collect Your Statistics and Celebrate Your Growth.

Every month, create a prize for your top inviter.

Skill Five: Collect

What Is Collecting?

Our second-to-last Karen's Friends and Fortune Flowchart skill involves intelligence gathering. Collecting information includes noticing, gathering data, and sharing insights with teammates. As they interact with the public and community members, your supporters gain information. Collecting this information allows you to respond and compete successfully.

Collecting begins with existing interactions. Your supporters notice, take notes, and share their findings. Here are some examples of assembled information and how nonprofits use it.

The development director realizes that almost all of your new donors ask the same three questions. You post a frequently asked question sheet on your website.

In the gift store, a staff member apologizes to fifteen people because you don't sell bottled water. You add water to your inventory.

Your board member attends an industry conference. The member returns with five solutions to a challenge. You schedule a pilot to test the top solution the following week.

Why Bother to Gather Intelligence?

We live in a data-driven world. Study after study of businesses reveals that people in direct contact with customers often know solutions to business challenges that remain elusive to managers. When it comes to information, nonprofit leaders fare somewhat better since they run leaner organizations.

Nonetheless, intelligence-gathering benefits nonprofits. Market insights allow you to respond to changing conditions quickly. Over time, collecting fuels excellence. You discover ways to save time and resources and generate new revenue. You improve your processes and produce better outcomes with fewer resources.

Collecting information also benefits the information collector in a way that will surprise you. To succeed in collecting, you must be present in the moment. You can't approach tasks like a zombie. Instead, you watch and listen carefully. You ask questions. You test your observations. As a result, even dull work becomes interesting.

How Does Collecting Information Help Fundraising?

When you collect, you often gain information that allows you to offer donors sweet-spot opportunities. You find new resources faster.

What Happens When We Forget to Collect?

You lose valuable, low-cost, and potentially high-impact information.

BEST PRACTICES

DOES COLLECTING WORK?

Here's a great example of collecting sponsor feedback. JL Bielon, executive director of the Lions Eye Institute for Transplant and Research, hosted a focus group of event sponsors. She asked for feedback about their experiences attending nonprofit galas. She learned several vital pieces of information including that the sponsors preferred tables that seated eight, not ten. This preference opened up seating for other paid attendees, and it saved JL the cost of two meals per sponsored table while she captured the same revenue. With this and other information, JL updated her sponsorship packages. You can collect similar material to enhance your revenue.

Skill Six: Introduce

The final Karen's Friends and Fortune Flowchart skill connects newcomers to others. You can also call introducing "handing off" or "connect bigger." You use this skill to help newcomers move from one relationship in your organization to many.

Introducing helps both individuals and the nonprofit by increasing connections. Connections make working together easier, fosters your community, and provides reasons to visit and participate in future events.

How Does Introducing Work?

Here's an example about engaging board members from my client work.

Before: The first time a new board member enters the boardroom, he or she only knows the board member who introduced him or her to the organization and the CEO. Six months later, when the inviting board member transfers to a new city, the nonprofit loses both the relocating member and the new member.

After: Using introducing before the first meeting, the current board member and the CEO will jot down points of connection between other members and the newcomer. At the first meeting, the inviting board member introduces the newcomer to Tom. "Both of you have new puppies, don't you?" Tom and the newcomer take it from there. They not only will remember each other at the next meetings, but every time they get together, they share dog stories. At the end of the first meeting, the newcomer meets and connects with three other members. More introductions take place in the months ahead.

What Happens When We Forget to Introduce?

Your organization's mission and success depends on ongoing relationships. When you fail to introduce people to others inside the organization, you limit your success.

How Does Introducing Help Fundraising?

Consistent use of this skill helps newcomers to enjoy a web of connections, instead of dangling from your cause by a single person. Successful connecting reduces the danger of severed relationships, such as those experienced by most nonprofits when beloved development staff members depart.

 BRING IT HOME

THREE CHEERS FOR YOUR SKILLS TOOLBOX

Before you beef up your organization's skills, establish a baseline so you can measure your progress. Using the Friends and Fortune Flowchart, rank how well members of your community use each of the six skills. Use a one-to-ten scale, with ten being the highest score. You can find a chart to use in the appendix or download a copy at *kedconsult.com/LetsRaiseMillions* (Password: together).

Choice and the Friends and Fortune Flowchart

The skills identified in the Friends and Fortune Flowchart catalog the most critical revenue development skills for nonprofits. You'll want to teach everyone all the skills and encourage their use. Beyond that, encourage everyone to find their favorites. Karen's rule is that everyone must help, but everyone *doesn't* have to contribute the same way. By offering choices, you'll maximize the odds that people will do what they love and become stars doing it.

Jack loves to tell stories. Jill loves to make guests feel at home. While they can each perform the other's favorite skill, you send Jill early to meetings to greet guests. You interrupt Jack's work for him to tell a story to tour groups.

"Love is a better master than duty," writes Peter Diamandis and Steven Kotler in their book *Abundance*. Choice honors peoples' self-knowledge and skills. Choice provides room for people to give their best.

Where Is the "Ask for Money" Skill?

Before I end this chapter, I want to answer a question about the flowchart. Where, you wonder, is the seventh skill? The one where your helpers ask their friends, relatives, and strangers to donate? I didn't include it.

Here's why. Asking for money is an advanced fundraising skill.

My number one rule about asking for money, and one I recommend for you to adopt, is that you only ask when you have a better than 50 percent chance of getting a yes. What's the best way to receive a donation? Plan your request. Answer these questions:

1. Amount: How much you will request?
2. Content: How you will use the money?
3. Timing: When you will ask?
4. People: Who is the best person to ask?

These questions require foresight, insight, and data. To maximize revenue, every nonprofit needs a central authority to answer these and similar questions. Too many clients have told horror stories of major gifts that were lost by a board or staff member asking for and receiving a minuscule gift. The returns of "making everyone ask" don't justify the costs.

Instead of asking everyone to request donations, enlist everyone to use the skills they like best to create a welcoming place where people volunteer to help financially. Let me explain what I mean. In a conversation, Judith Vredenburgh, president and CEO of Girls Inc., shared a story of a donor and eventual board member who *volunteered* to give $1 million in response to a $10 million challenge grant. The gift wasn't out of the blue. It was based on a long-term plan to help the donor and Girls Inc. reach mutual goals.

My philosophy aside, here's another reason not to include asking for money. The task scares people. Exempting them from asking for money will generate greater enthusiasm for other duties.

In the next chapter, I explore the oft used but infrequently explored phrase "relationship building." Can you guess the most important element of relationship building? Hold your answer until you remove the following from your to-do list.

 ## YOUR NOT-TO-DO TIP

REMOVE: DO IT ALL; INSERT: ONE SKILL AT A TIME

Resist the temptation to tackle getting your team to perform all the skills in the Friends and Fortune Flowchart at once. More is *not* always a good thing. Focus on one at a time. It's plenty.

I attended an event at the Yellowstone Institute on park geology. We began at 7:30 a.m. The schedule stated we'd finish by 5 p.m. At 2 o'clock, I garnered an underpinning of Yellowstone's enthralling geology—it was terrific. But by 3 p.m., the information began to run together. When the program closed at 6:30 p.m., I just wanted dinner.

Help others to improve one skill today. Tomorrow or next month, move to the following skill. It will be more than enough.

CHAPTER FOUR

RELATIONSHIP BUILDING: TRIED AND TRUE BLUEPRINTS

Olivia Thomas, the former executive director of Safe Place and Rape Crisis Center, Inc. (SPARCC), received a $100,000 surprise bequest. Olivia asked her board and staff if they knew the donor. No one did.

They checked their records. After an extensive search, they found the donor; a decade earlier, she purchased a T-shirt.

Is this another nonprofit random gift story? Might be, but probably not. Let me add what I've experienced when engaging with SPARCC. I've found the organization and its leaders exceptionally welcoming. The bequest is congruent with my SPARCC experience: the organization understands how to build enduring relationships.

At the epicenter of our ability to raise millions of dollars together lies our capacity to form quality relationships. Let's use our imagination to fill in the details on SPARCC's surprise bequest. In all likelihood, the donor cared about the organization's mission. Perhaps she was a survivor or had a friend or relative who endured domestic abuse. One day, she attended an event and stopped by a SPARCC booth. She bought a T-shirt. Inside it was tucked some literature. She went online and looked up the nonprofit. All the vetting pointed to SPARCC offering an outstanding investment. When she redid her will, she added SPARCC to it.

While the actual story probably involves more interactions than this tale, SPARCC's gift demonstrates the value of hosting. It shows you what you can gain by building the Friends and Fortune Flowchart infrastructure outlined in the last chapter.

The flowchart, however, is not the end-all. Even if you can get everyone to practice the six skills all the time, you aren't guaranteed bequests. Use of the skills doesn't ensure customers or secure donors. Instead, they help you to gather supporters.

What, then, do you need to do to obtain more donors and customers? To build relationships? What exactly does this mean? Throughout the nonprofit world, people use the phrase like it's a magic wand. This chapter dissects the nonprofit fundraising mantra "build a relationship" into specific activities. You do many of these activities now and you can do others before day's end. Ahead, you'll uncover a mix of mindsets and tactics to build on your current relationships and expertise and reach warmer, richer connections. This chapter is your relationship primer, based on decades of my experience in the nonprofit sector.

Let's start with an example. During her busy event, Angela, the founder of a giving circle, greeted me personally and shared why I should join the circle. When I joined, she called and invited me to breakfast to learn about my interests. When I attend meetings and volunteer, Angela warmly greets me and introduces me to other circle members. Are you surprised to learn that Angela's giving circle is quadruple the size of other local giving circles?

HOW TO BE A NETWORKING GURU

Building relationships starts with meeting people. I had the pleasure of leading a presentation with fellow networking experts recently. Here's a summary of the tips we shared about how to begin successful relationships when networking:

1. When you sign up for an event, note why you plan to attend in your calendar.

2. The day of the event, review your purpose.

3. When you arrive, no matter the traffic, if a loved one is at the doctor, or another calamity, *be* at the event. Remind yourself that you're attending to meet others and to help everyone achieve their goals.

4. When you meet someone new, use FORD questions. FORD is an acronym for Family and friends, Occupation, Recreation, and Dreams. For example, when the person you just met mentions their work, ask, "How did you end up doing that work?" (You can learn more about FORD online. Try Joshua Jamias's article on LinkedIn.)

5. Seek shared connections. Use the inventory in the following section for ideas.

6. Follow up within forty-eight hours. Reserve time after events to send emails and promised information.

INVENTORY OF COMMON CONNECTIONS FOR NETWORKING AND BEYOND

Find shared connections to build your relationships. Connections provide top-notch restart buttons for second and later meetings. For example, you could start a second conversation by asking if your contact has been back to visit your joint hometown. To help, here's a list of connections from my years of networking. I left room for you to add your ideas.

Locations

- shared hometown
- same home state
- live or lived in the same neighborhood
- traveled to or lived in the same locale
- sitting at the same table or sharing the same event small group
- _____
- _____

Affiliations

- attended the same college
- attended your relative's alma mater
- belong to the same political party
- favor a type of software, game, or social media
- attend or have attended the same or similar cultural activity
- prefer Apple or other electronic products
- love the same sport team
- support the same or related causes
- member or former member of the same sorority or fraternity
- choose the identical meal option or share special food needs (e.g., gluten-free)
- share the same faith, congregation, or denomination
- _____
- _____

Experiences

- experienced the same number of, or lack of, siblings
- played or participated in identical sports or clubs in school or at college
- worked at a comparable summer, part-time, or full-time job
- belong or belonged to the same group or club
- partake in the same preferred activity, such as boating, biking, or collecting stamps
- read comparable books or watched the same movie or online program
- tried an identical endurance or challenge activity, such as a ropes course
- like the same restaurants and type of food
- share a health condition
- both know someone with a rare health conditions
- express identical anxiety about the weather, getting the flu or the like
- share excitement about an upcoming event, such as the Super Bowl
- mutually committed to exercise, medication, or other activity
- prefer dogs over cats, or vice versa, or another pet
- _____
- _____

People

- like the same friends
- know former neighbors
- have children with a connection

- have children the same sex, age, or who share a trait
- have relatives who know each other
- _____
- _____

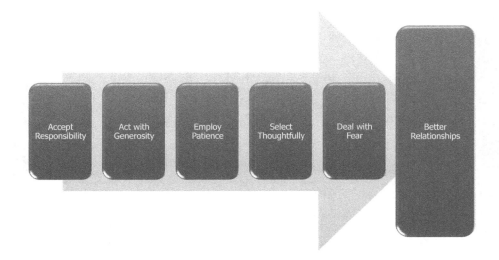

FIVE CRITICAL RELATIONSHIP HABITS

Excelling in the Space Between "Hello" and Your Thank-You Note

After you connect, how can you continue to move closer until you build a quality relationship? In the next section, you'll learn five critical relationship habits. They will, like a comfortable routine, help you to organize yourself, so you automatically prioritize your connections. You will use them to help you to nurture others over and over again.

Habit One: Embrace the Responsibility

Have you ever heard this advice? If you want people to attend your funeral, appear at theirs. This *is* illogical. If someone's dead, he or she won't come to your funeral. The wisdom contained in this quip nonetheless rings true. By demonstrating your concern for others, such as by attending funerals, people will attend to you.

This habit advises you to accept leadership in your relationships. That is, take the actions necessary to ensure that your connections bear fruit. Sometimes you attend funerals. Other times, you call, reach out, and risk being slightly annoying by following up a little too often.

For example, you lead by following up even when it's another's turn, it's been a long time, and it is awkward.

You save time following this habit. You don't have to decide if you will follow up. When the onus rests on your shoulders, you do.

Embracing the responsibility recognizes that you may need several actions to create the outcome you seek. Since one phone call, one email, or one text rarely makes enough noise in the market to get heard, you reach out, as needed, to connect.

One technique you can use is a habit I recommend to my clients, called Close the Loop. Here's how Close the Loop works. At the end of every exchange, you propose the next step. Close the Loop gives you a date and task to insert in your calendar. Let's look at a few examples.

With a Donor

Before: "Let's get together sometime."

Loop closing: "Let's have lunch next month. I'll send you several dates next week."

With a Customer

Before: "We're so glad you're considering this program for your child."

Loop closing: "We're so glad you're considering our program; I'll call you tomorrow to answer your follow-up questions."

With a Prospective Board Member

Before: "Great! I am so glad you're willing to consider joining the board."

Loop closing: "Great, I am so glad you're thinking it over. Would it be best if I called in a week or two, so you can share your thoughts?"

With a Visitor

Before: "We have a mailing list. Would you like to join it?"

After: "We'll send you our newsletter. You'll find it chock-full of great information."

IMPORTANT

HABIT TWO: ACT WITH GENEROSITY

When we're busy, we spend 95 percent of our time putting out fires, and 5 percent on the important task. By shifting your focus to the important things just 5 percent more of your time, you'll make tremendous progress.

Father Gregory J. Boyle, S.J., founder of Homeboy Industries in Los Angeles, a large gang intervention, rehabilitation, and reentry program, sums up the habit of generosity nicely, with this self-reminder: "Be here now."

When clients stop by Father Boyle's office, he uses the phrase like a mantra. To be present, he places his demanding agenda aside. He sets his mental musing on hold. He silences external distractions.

Boyle chooses now. Excellent relationships demand the same. The generosity habit calls us to grant others our full attention. Generosity involves your willingness to be present in our exchanges with others. Generosity reflects both health and capacity. It attracts others.

Simple words. Difficult to execute.

Why? You have a lot to do. You have multiple income streams to manage. You have a community to grow, and you're passionate about furthering your cause. For these and similar reasons, it's hard to be present.

Now for some good news. Filling your organization with generosity won't be as difficult as it sounds. Here's why:

1. Nonprofits spring from generosity. You were chartered to help others.

2. Generosity is contagious. It follows the rule of reciprocity. That is, if you're generous with me, I'm obligated to return your kindness.

3. You're motivated. You want generous vendors, staff members, volunteers, and donors.

Years ago, we lived on a forty-foot motorsailor in the Bahamas. One trip, we met Vern and Terry Kane. Since we'd been living afloat longer, we showed them several liveaboard tricks, including how to fish using bacon for bait. Before we sailed to different ports of call, Vern told us, "We always try to give more in our relationships then we get, but we couldn't do it with you."

We didn't intend to engage in a giving competition with the Kanes, but Vern succinctly expresses the spirit of generosity that made our relationship with the Kanes memorable twenty-five years later. Since you want everyone in your community to act generously, likewise seek to give more than you get.

Habit Three: Employ Patience

"Time can do what hurrying cannot." — Vicki Pugh, vice president for development at Palm Beach Atlantic University

Vicki's words remind you of the rewards of patience. You want, and often need, results now, but your donors and customers aren't ready. They need time to vet you, to come to a conclusion, and to act. You wait patiently because large gifts and purchases require more time than trinkets. You delay because forbearance can be a path to *yes*. You practice patience because you believe in your value.

Practicing patience means that while you prize action now, you recognize that often one of the most magical things you can do is wait. Waiting gives people space. Space conveys that you trust your prospect.

Furthermore, when you step back, your donors and customers might grow concerned that your offer will disappear. Someone else, a major gift donor fears, may get naming rights to Mom's building. Patience can inspire action because it kicks in FOMO, or the fear of missing out.

Regular use of patience generates a healthy perspective and alternatives. While you wait, you often discover other opportunities to pursue. You realize that your success doesn't depend on a single outcome.

Finally, before we move on to the next habit, I want to add some perspective. Using this habit recognizes that at some point, it's no longer your turn. Your prospective donor or customer *must* pick up the telephone, walk over your threshold, or text you to say "Yes."

How often should you reach out, and how long should you wait? Establish a rule that works for you. For many, it's three contacts in a work week before moving on to another option. For others, it's four times in seven working days. A sales professional told me that he contacted people fourteen times before giving up.

Whatever number or time you set, when you reach that number, as my yoga instructor tells us before relaxation, "Let go."

IMPORTANT

TIPS ON PRACTICING PATIENCE WHEN WAITING SEEMS IMPOSSIBLE

Find Alternatives. Mentally remove yourself from the sphere of needing a response *now.* Imagine you don't need the resources. What would you do then? Would you make the call? Send the email? Would you focus on a different project? Step back and you'll see new options.

Start the Other Options. A museum faced a $50,000 shortfall. The development team approached donors and shared the challenge. A second team planned how to avoid a future crisis. The program staff brainstormed ten low-cost ideas to generate cash flow. Three ideas succeeded and one closed the deficit. In the meantime, a donor made a substantial gift. All three efforts launched the organization into a financially sound new year. Begin other options.

Stand in Their Shoes. Envisage what it's like for the person on whom you wait. Mentally move so you can shift your gaze until you see the situation from their perspective. From here, consider what actions you will take to move forward.

Habit Four: Select Thoughtfully

Treating Everyone with Dignity Does Not Mean Treating Everyone the Same

Two new employees join your organization. Staff Member A eagerly participates in everything. She volunteers to lead new ventures and asks for more tasks. Her challenge? She finishes a fraction of what she starts. For instance, she misses submitting a grant by the deadline.

Staff Member B only accepts assignments and expresses doubt about her abilities to take on additional work. She begs not to lead a small group you assign. Her value to your organization? She finishes every task in an exemplary way, creating templates and processes to reuse. Her challenge? Evaluating the value of different jobs. Before writing thank you notes, she researches a donor who gave $50 for four hours.

You value fairness and equality. Do you, therefore, treat Staff Members A and B the same? Clearly no. You customize your treatment based on the individual's needs to help each staff member succeed. Staff Member A needs coaching to use more care selecting assignments and to be held accountable for completion. Staff Member B requires guidance to discern which tasks merit A+ efforts and which just need finishing.

You practice the habit of selecting thoughtfully when you focus your efforts on the activities and individuals that generate the most success, such as your best donors and prospects. For example, you plan to survey your 250 donors. You send the survey online to donors who give less than $100. You call the handful of individuals who gave between $101 and $999. You invite donors who gave between $1,000 and $2,500 to a focus group. Finally, you ask everyone who gave more than $2,500 the questions in a personal meeting.

Selecting thoughtfully conflicts with the traditional nonprofit mindsets. Nonprofits love equality. Sit down at most staff meetings in most nonprofits, and you discover collective decision-making at work. We like unanimous decisions. Moreover, many parts of the sector fight against inequality.

To succeed in building long-term relationships that lead to major gifts, this habit guides you to treat everyone with respect. It also calls for you to recognize the fact that year in, year out, 10 percent of the folks in your community will provide 90 percent of your resources. In short, even though everyone has a role in generating funds for your organization, not every action or person yields similar results.

Habit Five: Deal with Fear

What keeps nonprofits from achieving more of their mission and flying toward their vision? Fear. Nonprofits fear to ask. Donors fear to give. Customers fear making buying commitments. The final relationship habit recognizes fears.

Using the habit, you recognize the presence of fear and act to reduce it. For instance, since people will make mistakes as they experiment with new behaviors, you shield them from the consequences of beginning errors so they can build skills, allowing them practice time. Furthermore, since asking for help involves the risk of rejection, you soften any rejections by offering perspective and reminding people that relationships wax and wane.

THE FEAR OF FUNDRAISING AND PUBLIC SPEAKING

Despite its common citation, people are *not* more afraid of speaking in public than of death. (This claim stems from faulty research.) In fact, most people prefer public speaking to asking friends for money. Therefore, you're on solid ground if you assume your supporters fear fundraising.

Help them to cure this anxiety. How? Nudge them to practice the fundraising skills included in Karen's Friends and Fortune Flowchart. Also, *never* ask for fundraising help. Instead, make specific requests. "Bobby, will you issue six invitations to friends and follow up with them twice about attending next month's event?"

Over time, some of your community members will discover that they love fundraising. How will this happen? They'll gain skills and confidence. Plus, their mindsets will change when they see the results.

Fear and Its Disguises

Often when you're afraid, you don't even know it. For instance, you have an upcoming meeting with a donor. You notice a tickle in your throat. You think, *Should I cancel the meeting? I'm not sure the donor's all that interested. Maybe they said yes to meet because they're lonely. I don't want to give them strep throat.* If you continue in this vein, you'll cancel. If you stop and see that fear is behind your doubts and scratchy throat, you'll go.

Anticipate reluctance, complaining, and excuses when you engage others in raising resource tasks. Before you respond, assume fear is at work.

I led a staff retreat for a legal organization experiencing declining revenue. The board and CEO created a strategy to build their donations to offset the loss of government funds. They asked staff to support this effort using many of the techniques shared in this book.

Early in the retreat, one of the lawyers stood up and said, "I didn't get in this organization to fundraise." He voiced what many in the room felt: "Fundraising is *not* our job."

The fact, however, was that without new income, everyone in the room would be unemployed. Once the staff saw the logic of the change, I conducted an exercise to help them to name their fundraising fears. By day's end, the lawyer who objected shared that while he wasn't thrilled, he would give "this funding stuff a try." The next quarter, the nonprofit's donated income grew by 30 percent over the previous year.

It's likely that the people in your community will also sing "It's not my job." What can you do? Here are five responses, from the easy to challenging, from proactive to reactive.

1. Include income development in all job descriptions for all positions including volunteers, the board, and staff.

2. Inform newcomers that everyone helps with income development.

3. Design specific tasks for each role or individual to support resource development. Measure actions. Praise successful task completion. Celebrate outcomes.

4. Discover what skills or resources people need to become proficient. Offer them.

5. Consistently lead the charge. Prove, by your actions, that you will stick with this effort despite the clamor of other demands.

To excel in the time between *hello* and *thank you*, embrace the responsibility, act with generosity, employ patience, select thoughtfully, and deal with fears. These five critical relationship habits will help you develop relationships that bring new resources to your door.

In this chapter, so far, you've read about networking and the five habits. In the next section, you'll learn about how to insert joy into the relationships you're building, especially existing ones.

 BRING IT HOME

MASTERING THE FIVE
CRITICAL RELATIONSHIP HABITS

Do the five habits seem overwhelming? What I learned from working with nonprofit leaders is that most organizations practice these habits already. Is this true for you? Find out with this exercise.

Below you will find a table that lists the habits. Rank your organization on how often you practice each habit, on the one-to-ten scale. Choose one, if you rarely see this action. Note a ten if the habit reflects standard procedures. Mark a star next to the behavior you'd most like to improve in the goal column. Jot down five ways you might close the gap in the last column. Pick one to start today.

Habits	Current Rank	Goal	Actions to Close Gap
1. Accept Responsibility			
2. Act with Generosity			
3. Practice Patience			
4. Select Thoughtfully			
5. Recognize Fear			

INSERT JOY INTO EXISTING RELATIONSHIPS

Renewal Recipes for Refreshed Relationships with Donors, Supporters, and More

"This is so much fun; I'm having a blast." —a board member

You meet someone and connect. You made a good impression and you left the gathering feeling good. When you chatted, you discovered commonalities. Perhaps you discussed a favorite movie, found the same argument in the lecture compelling, or realized your sisters have the same name. New meetings that uncover commonalities spiral upward with each connection.

Unfortunately, later meetings often fail to provide a comparable boost. When meeting again, both parties often make less effort to establish a good impression. Subsequent sessions tend to focus on tasks, building connection takes a back seat.

How can you change this downward dynamic and move it upward again? My favorite relationship-growing secret sprang from a conversation several years ago. Unfortunately, I can't remember who shared the advice.

Here's the secret. Overcome later meeting doldrums by pretending your second meeting's another first encounter. To help your imagination, move to a fresh venue. Take a walk together. Join your contact in their favorite coffee shop. Invite them to sit with you at a luncheon. Ideally, meet your connection doing something *they* love to do.

Can't change venues? You're not doomed to the doldrums. You can regain freshness by investing a few minutes exploring new shared connections. For ideas, review the Shared Connection Inventory before your meeting.

WORDS AND RELATIONSHIPS: SAYING WHAT MATTERS

Let's explore relationships focusing on specific words we use with others. While researchers tell us that we convey more information by our bodies and our tones than words, words still constitute an essential part of communications. My favorite word secrets come next.

Practice Brevity

Brevity saves time. Here are some full sentences to use in conversations, emails, texts, and elsewhere. Use these short sentences often:

- Yes.
- No.

- Thank you.
- Got it.
- Wonderful.
- Let's discuss at our meeting.
- See you soon.

Brevity in conversation allows the other person to talk more. Since most people want to speak more than listen, the briefer you are, the happier they'll be.

Practice giving concise answers of twenty-five words or less. Post a sticky on your computer, with the number "25" on it to remind yourself of this goal. This limit requires you to spend a few seconds thinking before speaking. With practice, brevity takes less time and effort and gets the job done. Moreover, modeling brevity encourages others to adopt it, saving time throughout your organization.

Use Templates

You're answering a board member's question when you realize that you answered the same issue last week. You search through the five hundred emails, find that response, and paste it into your reply. You can continue to scrounge, cut, and paste. Or you can create a set of frequently asked questions templates.

Make the thought "I've answered this before" a cue to create a reusable template. Label and file the document. Then use as needed.

Collect Power Phrases

Don't underestimate the power of the right words to save the day. What's a power phrase? Here's an example from the book *Never Split the Difference:* "Have you given up on this project?" I use this question after someone tells me a project's a high priority and yet my telephone calls get ignored. According to author Chris Voss, this phrase works because it provides the recipient control. Moreover, the words suggest your pending withdrawal. Since we all hate to lose anything, you find this power phrase helps people to reprioritize your relationship.

The question "Have you given up on this project?" is only one of many words, phrases, and questions to use in correspondence, conversations, and meetings to generate results. Here's an example to close meetings: "What are the three most important decisions we made?" While you probably made more than three decisions, asking attendees to identify the top ones helps everyone to focus on the central themes. Furthermore, it ends the meeting with a sense of accomplishment. That's a lot of work for nine words to accomplish! You'll find power phrases so helpful, you'll want to collect them.

Four Ways to Grow Your Power Phrases

Power phrases are like good books, you can never have too many. Here's how to begin a collection.

- Listen to your own words. Record phrases that worked.

- Listen to interviews. Jot down expressions to repeat.

- Highlight phrases from your subsector. Massage these into your verbal and print messages.

- Ask presenters how they would respond to a question. Document their exact words.

- Study books, articles, and other materials. Note any techniques you like.

Once you have a collection, you'll want to organize the phrases to retrieve and use them. I record phrases on my iPhone so I can review them before meetings.

Weave your power phrases into your conversation and correspondence. At first, they may feel awkward. Don't worry. Your listener won't know it's new to you. Moreover, you'll be amazed at their effectiveness.

FIVE WAYS TO FOLLOW UP WITHOUT STALKING

With so many relationships, it's only natural that you'll let some of them lapse. After long breaks, reconnecting feels uncomfortable. Nonetheless, if you'd like to reconnect, how can you comfortably make the next move? In this section, I provide specific tactics to rekindle relationships. Use them like power switches to send fresh energy and spark your connections to life.

1. Leave a Breadcrumb Trail

Hansel and Gretel dropped a trail of breadcrumbs to find their way back home. During blizzards, farmers tied ropes around their waists to get between their home and the barn to milk their cows. Likewise, plan a path to reconnect. For instance, end your coffee meeting by saying, "So let's have coffee again after the first of the year." When your coffee partner agrees, you've made it your responsibility to set the next appointment.

2. Pick Your Best Excuse

You failed to leave a breadcrumb trail. What else can you do? Use an excuse. You call, for instance, and share why the contact was at the top of your mind. You say, "I was thinking of you because___."

In my experience, we worry too much about the *quality* of our excuses. I've discovered that for most people, any excuse will do. Your explanation can be as flimsy as "I saw your name on a file." It can be elaborate as "I read an article I wanted to share." It doesn't matter. Most people are genuinely glad to hear from you.

3. Check a Fact

Your alma mater hires a student to call alumni and asks them to update their records. This request renews relationships—without stalking. You can call for a fact before sending an email, your latest newsletter, or an article. Yes, checking a fact is a type of picking your best excuse.

To use this technique, you must *need* the information. Otherwise, you're connecting under fast pretenses and sending your relationships down a shoddy pathway. If the recipient suspects you're fibbing, you'll cause more damage than you gain restoring the relationship. Use this tactic with care.

4. Future Travel

"I'll be in the area and be happy to stop by." This old sales technique works to contact old acquaintances. You will find it succeeds, even if you're visiting from the next town over. You'll want to avoid using the cliché. Instead, share that you'll be nearby and invite them to meet for coffee.

5. Seek Advice

My final recommendation on the best ways to reconnect works by itself and in combination with picking your best excuse. For example, you call a contact and mention that you just saw their name. It reminded you that you wanted to ask for their advice.

In my experience, these reconnecting techniques work nearly 100 percent of the time when used with one caveat: make it your goal to provide new value. You'll read more about value in the next chapter. Now, here's another time-saving recommendation.

YOUR NOT-TO-DO TIP

BE PRESENT FOR FIVE

Carnus was a low-functioning adult. He hauled trash for a living. Every summer afternoon around 3 o'clock, he would stop by the office of the church where he worshiped. Wet with sweat from head-to-toe, Carnus would head to the water cooler, drink several glasses, and plop himself into a visitor chair. He'd stay until closing, enjoying air conditioning and staff camaraderie.

Joanne, whose desk was nearest to Carnus's seat, didn't want to be rude, but she had work to do. The pastor offered this brilliant advice. "Spend five minutes with him. Be present. Then go back to work." The hard part of this advice is being fully present for five minutes. However, in just five minutes, you can make a superior connection.

Give five minutes to staff, clients, customers, and donor. Be brief. Be present for five. Then, be off.

CHAPTER FIVE

DEVELOPING THE NEW PHILANTHROPIC ORGANIZATION

A t a beach wedding three days after Christmas, the priest dropped the ring into the soft sand. The wedding party and the guests fell to their knees and pawed the ground as beach walkers stopped to gawk.

Five minutes passed, then six.

Nothing.

A child in swim trunks stepped out from the crowd, holding a toy metal detector. The child swung the wand back and forth over the sand.

Silence. Then a single beep. Followed by a trill of beeps. The priest swept the sand away and triumphantly held up the ring.

The ceremony began again—only to be stopped again by the groom's father, who was following the child and trying to give him a $20 bill to keep the toy stocked with batteries.

Nonprofits often beg—in socially acceptable ways—for money. We forget that money follows value.

When people experience your value, like the groom's father, they'll chase after you to give you resources. The child wasn't seeking a tip. He was feeling powerful being a hero and enjoying his toy.

To raise millions for your nonprofit, offer value. Not only will the results help you to achieve your mission, but you'll also give people the chance to change lives. Like the child on the beach, your community wants to feel powerful, and heroic—and they will pay for the privilege.

 LOCATION CHECK

WHERE ARE WE?

So far, you've learned that you can build a sustainable nonprofit organization. You were introduced to your triple bottom lines and learned about vision. After exploring different philanthropic income opportunities, you discovered techniques for building your community. Finally, you learned some new ideas about establishing quality relationships.

In the first half of this chapter, you'll discover how to build your new philanthropic organization around value. Then—before moving on to the specific roles of your board, staff, vendors, and others in the next part of the book—you'll discover a fresh take on the concepts of fundraising, development, and philanthropy that will help you to invite people to partake and create value before moving on to the specific roles of your board, staff, vendors, and others.

WHAT IS VALUE?

"Make him an offer he can't refuse." —*The Godfather*

There are numerous definitions of value. Here's one to note: value is the usefulness, importance, or worth of something to others.

On one level, you're already a value expert. You know that to identify what's valuable to others, it helps to "get into their shoes"—that is, to see what you offer from another perspective.

It's hard to remember to do this. For instance, the president of a statewide organization complained by saying, "We were part of a national organization that substantially increased the dues without providing additional value. We're no longer members."

From the outside, you recognize that increasing dues without increasing value is a losing proposition. However, as a sector, we are often guilty of doing things like this to our donors. We receive a donation and send a perfunctory thank you. Shortly afterwards we request a more substantial gift without proposing additional value.

 BRING IT HOME

WHY DO YOUR DONORS, CUSTOMERS, AND VOLUNTEERS VALUE YOU?

Ask a dozen volunteers, customers, and donors: "Why us?" That is, why did you get involved in this organization? Record and study the answers to discover your value.

Your Three-Step Money Solution

How can you use value to increase your organization's revenue? Here's the quick answer:

1. Identify your value.
2. Identify who needs it *and* has the resources to gain it.
3. Communicate to them the opportunity to obtain your value.

The first half of this chapter focuses on identifying and expanding your value.

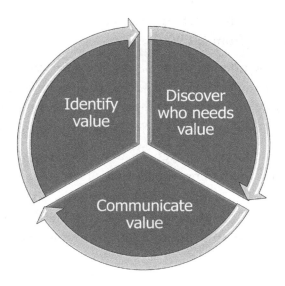

Your Valuable Organization

Your value is unique to you. Determining your value allows you to offer unique products and services. Even if you have a hundred nonprofit competitors in your neighborhood, none of them delivers precisely what you do. Your value helps you to stand out and avoid becoming a commodity, or just another nonprofit seeking support.

TO INCREASE YOUR REVENUE, NAME YOUR VALUE

Your cause is worthy of big, massive, and even colossal investment. Your success in collecting large repeat investments depends on identifying your benefits. To tap your value, know it.

Do you know all of your value? Maybe. Maybe not. In workshops, exploring this concept, I've had people tell me that they've assumed their supporters are just like them. That is, that everyone loves their cause for the same reasons. While it's fun to get jazzed up about the same things, if you assume you're connecting because of the same aspect of your work, you're inhibiting your resource growth.

Life is complex. People find lots of different benefits in your work. This diversity is good news. It provides you with more opportunities to deliver value, probably more than you've considered so far.

In an expert conversation, Michael Pastreich, the former CEO of the Florida Orchestra, shared that most of the orchestra's donors found value in three distinct areas: (1) they loved music, (2) they loved what the orchestra offers youth, (3) they believed that every quality community supports a thriving orchestra. In other words, they valued the orchestra's role in providing a high-quality community life.

Let's translate these areas into universal nonprofit benefits. You provide value because of:

- what your organization does for individuals;
- what you do for others;
- what your nonprofit does for all of us.

You can use these three ideas as broad categories to start your organization's list of the value you offer. Don't stop with these three values. Keep going. To inspire you and to help you increase your revenue, I've crafted a list of values that nonprofits provide. You'll find them after Citizens School's best practices.

BEST PRACTICES

CAN YOU CRACK AN INTRACTABLE SOCIAL PROBLEM AND YOUR INTRACTABLE MONEY CHALLENGE AT THE SAME TIME?

Citizen Schools, headquartered in Boston, helps adolescents from low-income communities to explore new fields, learn new skills, and build a foundation for their future. It creates these results and more by creating volunteer teachers, often middle managers from corporations.

What value does Citizen Schools provide? The program benefits students, their classrooms, families, and more.

Emily McCann, CEO of Citizen Schools, shared a unique value that helps drive the organization's sponsorship revenue. When corporations partner with Citizen Schools, they gain the traditional nonprofit sponsorship benefit, such as branding, employee engagement, and for long-term thinkers, access to potential employees from diverse backgrounds.

However, that's not all. The program helps corporations to improve their diversity efforts, as defined by race and ethnicity. The relationships that volunteers develop with students create pathways that break down assumptions that exist across communities. After teaching at Citizen Schools, employees are more likely to pave the way for students of color to participate as interns and to support diverse employees who join their companies.

You just read a surprising twist on a value that Citizen Schools brings corporate partners: employees learn how to succeed in an increasingly diverse world. As you read about Citizen Schools, did you realize that you offer something similar? Do you run a program that helps volunteers to understand diversity? Alternatively, do you provide another just as compelling value? No matter what you find, if you're unaware that you create a benefit, it's unlikely you'll share it with potential partners and even more unlikely you'll gain rewards for creating that value.

Knowing your value in the eyes of those willing to partner with you will help to grow your bottom line. When you know your value, you'll share it with people seeking what you offer. You'll improve how you deliver it. Your partners will be prepared to receive it. If you don't know your value, it's a bit like sending a turkey to a friend's house for Thanksgiving without knowing they'll be home to receive it.

TURBOCHARGE YOUR VALUE: THE DAVIS VALUE INVENTORY LIST
Sixty-Six Values

You offer way more value than you imagine *now*. Below is a generic inventory of sixty-six benefits you might currently offer your donors, customers, board members, staff, vendors, or others. I added room for you to add new values.

You'll note I divided the list into the three value categories:

- what your organization does for individuals,
- what you do for others, and
- what you do for all of us.

Use this list to step out of your historical thinking and explore possibilities. After the inventory, you'll read about two additional values that every nonprofit offers.

What You Do for Everyone

Create Change

- right a wrong
- improve a situation
- solve a problem
- streamline a process
- cure a disease
- use limited resources effectively
- build resources and future capacity
- change a culture
- end suffering
- make the world safer
- model how to change a culture
- offset waste or loss
- change or improve lives
- stimulate creativity
- encourage innovation
- reduce feeling of helplessness
- evoke sweet memories
- experience the cute and whimsical
- give hope
- model collective and humanitarian action
- _____
- _____

What You Do for Others

Protect and Uplift the Vulnerable

- improve the environment for future generations
- protect pets, endangered species, and other creatures
- teach children and youth
- improve human bodies
- help victims
- assist seniors
- help families and individuals in crisis
- help the unemployed and underemployed
- change or improve specific individuals' lives
- _____
- _____

What You Do for Me

Gain Knowledge, Expertise, and Information

- understand a mission in depth
- obtain curated information
- understand "the system" before improving it
- discover ways to create scale
- identify what not to do
- learn leadership skills
- gain experience using specific skills
- discover how nonprofits win sponsorships, donations, and grants
- participate in thoughtful response to a traumatic event
- develop interpersonal and group process skills
- _____
- _____

Entertain

- fill spare time by offering activities for vacation and other hours
- stimulate laughter
- hear stories
- learn for learning's sake
- participate in adult play experiences
- experience the world in fresh ways
- _____
- _____

Belong

- join a community
- connect with simpatico others
- establish new and renewed contacts
- meet potential business referrals
- partake in a large group effort
- find people with similar challenges
- _____
- _____

Tactical

- fulfill an obligation or return a favor
- confirm one's identity as a philanthropist
- experience a convenience
- establish a giving habit by making monthly contributions
- receive tax deductions
- obtain insider benefits, such as discounts
- help heirs to learn philanthropy to avoid "wealth ruin"

- improve the community
- improve wealth
- _____
- _____

Accomplishment

- practice philanthropy
- check an action off a list
- please authority figures, dead or alive ("Mom would be proud")
- honor used goods
- reduce an annoyance
- _____
- _____

Two More Not-to-Forget Values to Add to Your Inventory

You Exist

In hunting for value, you might focus on our fulfilling your mission, services, events, branding, tax-reduction opportunities, and the like. When you do, you might miss out on a significant value: your existence.

At a session I led with the Arts and Business Council of Miami, the participants discussed the values they offered sponsors. A member of the audience shared the highlights of his table's discussion. He said, "We talked about not forgetting that people sponsor the arts because it gives them the chance to be with artists and catch the creative vibe."

Besides being a brilliant thing for the cultural institutions to remember, the essence of his point holds for all nonprofits. You give your community members the opportunity to do good work. Even when they're not actively working, they know that good work is still underway. In other words, you provide value because you exist.

Philanthropy Grows Wealth

Did you know that decades of research prove that philanthropic activity increases the wealth of people who give? The relationship is causal. That it, it doesn't stem from the fact that people with means have more to give. Giving actually increases wealth.

Yes, this is counterintuitive. Think about why it's true. Philanthropy improves our social bonds. It connects us to others. Giving offers us a greater sense of safety. Researchers believe that giving helps people to be happier, and happier people experience more agency. That is, when you give to others, you feel powerful. Over time, you use your agency to act. Acting increases wealth.

Philanthropy grows wealth. This is the second not-to-forget value to add to your inventory. Remember it. Share it. This fact will offer comfort to those who fear to ask and to those who fear they have too little to give.

How Can You Use the Davis Value Inventory List to Its Full Benefit?

Here are several ways to use the Davis Value Inventory List.

Take the Inventory

Go through the inventory. Mark the values that your organization provides during a typical year. Share the list with your staff. Ask them to look for other benefits that you offer. Explore any surprise answers. Give the inventory to your board. Ask them to pick the top five values that they obtain from being associated with your organization. Challenge them to name three values that aren't on the list.

Toss it—Initially

Here's another way to use the list: skip it. Instead, write your own list. To do this, dissect your activities into their value components.

For instance, your first-time, Saturday morning build-site volunteers at Habitat for Humanity benefit from the chance to:

- improve the housing stock
- help a family
- learn skills
- improve their sense of power to create change
- learn the Habitat story
- participate in a physical work
- meet and work with others
- try something new
- receive expressions of gratitude

Once you write your list, return to the value inventory. Add any missing values to it.

With the knowledge you gain by inventorying your value, you'll be in a better position to market your opportunities. You can also design your activities to provide more benefits. Getting value once is great. Obtaining it consistently provides you the means to obtain revenue repeatedly.

THE VALUE OF PHILANTHROPY, DEVELOPMENT, AND FUNDRAISING

With your values inventoried, let's double back and explore the value of philanthropy, development, and fundraising. Nonprofits use these three terms interchangeably, even though each carries a distinct meaning. Sloppy use confuses supporters and, over time, decreases revenue.

Over 80 percent of the general public doesn't understand fundraising and development and how they link to philanthropy. My educated guess, based on decades of experience, is that if your nonprofit struggles with earning revenue, people around you aren't clear on the concepts either.

What people fail to understand is that fundraising and development consist of, as Janet Boguch with Non-Profit Works explains, "...not just asking for money, it is a set of strategies carried out continuously and systematically to bring resources to the organization."

Illuminating Philanthropy, Development, and Fundraising

Philanthropy is using personal resources to help others. Philanthropy, when designed well, benefits both the giver and the recipient. We all have the potential to be more philanthropic. We start here:

With support, we grow:

Development is the process nonprofits use to help people to grow as philanthropists. The line drawn between the small and the large hearts represents how nonprofits create a highway that invites their supporters to move from little to big philanthropy.

Fundraising is a collection of opportunities that nonprofits offer to allow their supporters to express their philanthropy. These include giving envelopes in your mailer, your wine and cheese party, and a lunch meeting where you share major gift needs. Your fundraising activities are designated on the image below with the vertical lines. Fundraisers serve as entrance ramps to your development superhighway.

GETTING CLEAR ON PHILANTHROPY, FUNDRAISING, AND DEVELOPMENT

Share these illustrations and definitions with your staff, board, and other supporters. Encourage everyone to use precise language.

You can download a poster, using the password *together*, at *kedconsult. com/LetsRaiseMillions*

Actions Around Philanthropy, Development, and Fundraising

Too many nonprofit supporters believe that obtaining resources, especially money, to run a nonprofit is a necessary evil. After all, the real work is the mission. Why risk, they think, going over to "the dark side"? In a session on Entrepreneurial Nonprofit Leadership, an audience member asked, "Is it possible to run a nonprofit and not to be focused on money?"

Mention fundraising to staff, board members, and volunteers, and some in the crowd will raise their hands, palms outward like a cop stopping traffic, and say, "I don't do fundraising." Others look longingly at the door, at the table, and their cell phones. Many would rather have a mammogram, root canal, or even perhaps give their own eulogy than to fundraise. Asking for donations, in their opinion, is akin to begging in the street—only one gets to dress better.

At the same time, a collective belief exists that fundraising, although distasteful, can be bought. It's not that hard. Just as you call a plumber to fix your commode, to obtain donations, you need an expert. If plumbers went on strike, people reason, after watching YouTube, they'd fix their commodes. Like plumbing, they think, fundraising requires skills, an inborn talent to like something that sounds unpleasant—skills they don't believe they have and don't want to learn.

Beliefs like these whirl around and interact in nonprofits with astonishing regularity and create serious consequences. Collectively, they form roadblocks to obtaining income. For some, growing revenue represents nonprofit survival. For others, access to income provides the opportunity to launch their work to the next level of excellence to reach their visions.

Do Your Supporters Get Fundraising, Development, and Philanthropy?

Yes, your supporters understand giving, especially when it comes to the reasons they give. "I give," shares a donor, "to a camp I attended. It meant a lot to me, and I hope to provide the experience to others."

Do your supporters get fundraising, development, and philanthropy? Not so much when it comes to understanding how to motivate others to give to your nonprofits and how it provides them value.

Everyone can benefit from greater clarity about fundraising, development, and philanthropy. Most importantly, approaching potential donors with a fresh understanding will increase donations and improve repeat gifts.

THE NEW PHILANTHROPIC ORGANIZATION: HELPING PEOPLE UNDERSTAND THAT FUNDRAISING IS NOT A DIRTY WORD

How you and those around you think about fundraising tremendously impacts your success. Fundraising—that is, the set of opportunities you offer people to express their philanthropy, specifically to support your mission—helps others. This definition focuses on the people giving for *their* benefit. Fundraising, therefore, is about service.

Is this how most people think about fundraising? Sadly, no.

Lacking a magic wand to more quickly transform your organization, how about brain surgery for your board and staff? Imagine it now. You gather predawn in the presurgery waiting room, dressed in a skimpy gown with an opening down the back. En masss, you reluctantly climb onto icy gurneys. A team of surgical staff dressed head-to-toe in green rolls your group into the frigid operating room.

Just before the anesthesiologist places the masks over your faces, the surgical team reads the checklist. Since this is an unusual process, and a *little* extreme, the team asks an additional question: "Are you enthused about asking people who love your organization to help support it?"

For the patients who shout, "Yes!" the surgery staff steps back, apologizes for the misunderstanding, and sends the patient for breakfast.

For the patients who respond negatively, the anesthesiologist approaches mask in hand, and the operation begins. During surgery, the surgeon inserts a microrecorder in each cranium that whispers, "Their goals. Their goals…" How does this help? When you remember that obtaining resources involves helping others to reach *their* goals, you focus on creating mutual value.

The surgeon also suctions, as necessary, any anxiety the patient has concerning talking about money to give your team confidence and peace of mind. Once everyone recovers, you discover new enthusiasm for obtaining resources. People see what they've never seen before. They find it's an honor to offer your community opportunities to help a nonprofit achieve its mission and to help community members meet their goals.

Is such a change possible? Yes, and without surgery.

In the pages that follow, you'll learn about how different actions from CEOs, staff members, the board of directors, volunteers, and others will help you to raise revenue. Imagine what similar excitement among your supporters will do to grow your revenue!

 YOUR NOT-TO-DO TIP

STOP ASKING PEOPLE TO FUNDRAISE

When you ask for help, avoid the word *fundraise*. Call it "growing the community," "inviting people to get involved," or "finding out what people value." Use the word fundraising to praise. "Your work engaging that couple shows your great fundraising skills." Why? What you mean by fundraising and what others hear are worlds apart. Until you bridge the gap, don't ask for fundraising help.

PART II
RAISING MILLIONS TOGETHER ROLE BY ROLE

You're well on your way to developing a new philanthropic organization. You believe it's possible. You understand how to build it. In the chapters you've read and the exercises you've done (you *have* done the exercises, right?), you gained the language and tools to help explain to others a culture of philanthropy and how you will raise millions together.

Just like sports leaders who generate fan nations, you can create communities filled with raving fans that help fundraise. In the chapters ahead, I share how to help people in and around your nonprofit to fall in love with fundraising. How will you get your board engaged? How can you help the staff to get it? How might you get your donors, vendors, and others to participate? The journey from here on gets specific on the *together* in the title of this book.

CHAPTER SIX

BOARD HEROES: CREATING WORLD-CLASS AMBASSADORS

"In terms of helping you to obtain income, how do you rate your board, from one to one hundred?" I asked. "With one being, "we need to hold a garage sale," and ninety and above reflecting giving substantial help obtaining revenue."

"Ten."

The question asked of a wide variety of nonprofit leaders often yields the same or similarly troubling answers. In a recent survey of sixty-six Meals on Wheels executives, this question generated an average score of forty-five. Another study of 2,700 CEOs and development directors found that "three out of four executive directors say that board members are not doing enough to support fundraising." To succeed at maximizing your revenue, your nonprofits need the help of your board. Many nonprofits don't get this help.

Can you turn your board of directors into supporters, and even champions, in the revenue development process? Yes. To learn how to create board champions, read on.

WHY DO YOU NEED YOUR BOARD'S HELP TO DEVELOP RESOURCES?

Getting your board smitten with fundraising delivers tremendous advantages. Besides budget growth, boards help close gifts and sell products and services. This section explores specific ways that board engagement in resource development bumps up nonprofit success.

Boards that engage spread your work deep into the community. Your board knows lots of people. They have rich and diverse relationships with their neighbors, professional acquaintances, congregations, social groups, clubs, chambers, vendors, PTAs, and the like. Furthermore, your board members can help you to meet these people. By recruiting well, you can attend every critical gathering in town.

Moreover, you select board members because they're leaders. The combination of their circulation in the community and their leadership skills makes your board members especially adroit at helping you to reach your Magic Circle of Next.

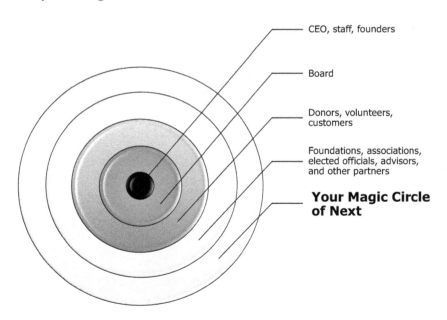

CEO, staff, founders

Board

Donors, volunteers, customers

Foundations, associations, elected officials, advisors, and other partners

Your Magic Circle of Next

Great board members help you to meet prospective donors and customers. They also remain perpetual outsiders. Even if your board members volunteer daily at your organization, they retain their outsider perspective because they can quit volunteering in an instant.

Their continuous outside viewpoint allows them to experience everything you do differently. They understand and express their experiences through different filters. You can, for instance, ask a board member, "Is this something you would invest in?" and obtain a quantitatively different answer than you'd receive from one of your managers, the local community foundation, a vendor, or your mother. Your staff, for instance, may think it's a grand idea to invite your sponsors for a three-hour tour. A board member who has been on half a dozen nonprofit tours would advise you to limit all tours to thirty minutes.

Moreover, board members with a business background offer more. Since they frequently visit intersections where commerce takes place, they understand why and how people exchange cash and resources to obtain value. Nonprofit leaders, because of their service emphasis, find themselves less in tune with these commercial mindsets.

Sponsorships provide a perfect example. As you prepare to meet two sponsors, your board member who has business connections with them can tell you, "Joe's an immediate bottom-line kind of guy. Ashley, in contrast, thinks more about long-term investments." With Joe, you emphasize outcomes this year. With Ashley, you stress building long-term connections. You win both sponsorships.

Finally, because your board members fulfill many different roles in their lives, including board service, they must, because of the press of their obligations, be choosey. The connections they secure are likely to be of high value to your nonprofit. Their discernment, born of too much to do, is good news. You don't want to connect with *everyone*.

You seek a handful of people with the most potential to care about and engage in your work, and in turn, be thrilled that someone invited them to get involved.

Board members, because of their time constraints and leadership gifts, are in the ideal position to help you find the 10 percent of people who will create 90 percent of the impact you seek.

  BEST PRACTICES

SMART RECRUITMENT STRATEGY

When Tracey Galloway began as CEO at Community Cooperative, she built a board by seeking individuals of different ages, interests, and neighborhoods to reach the entire community. The result? The nonprofit regularly has a representative at almost every meeting in Lee County, Florida. Besides connecting to others, her board members gather information, seek opportunities, discover community needs, and look for people with a potential passion for the cooperative's mission.

What's in It for Them?

Why Your Board Members Hope You Will Ask Them to Help with Resource Development

This section explores the value that board members gain when they help you to grow resources, but first, a little preamble. With 1.5 million nonprofits with all kinds of origins, funding streams, and purposes, you'll struggle to locate a "typical board." In the United States, some boards get appointed by governors. Others include founders, lifetime members, or clients. Some members join in response to their passion, others because their job requires serving somewhere. Many boards include experienced leader; others mostly include individuals in their first position. In short, when you meet one board—you've met one board.

Therefore, not everything you read below may work for your board. Nonetheless, most of it can be adapted to your circumstances. Despite the differences, there are great commonalities in the values that individual board members gain by accepting philanthropic, development, and fundraising roles.

I divided the benefits into two groups. The first benefits focus on how helping to raise resources impacts how members see themselves, their skills, and the world—what I call "board selfies." The second benefit group involves how others perceive your members—"board groupies."

In total, the benefits that board members can acquire are so strong that you'd be remiss not to share opportunities for them to help. Read and digest that message. Reflect and incorporate it into your thinking. Doing so will help you to invite new members with confidence.

As Kathy Kingston writes in *A Higher Bid*, "Board members *are* eager to help the nonprofit they support, but most of them don't feel comfortable raising money.... they often feel totally unequipped, afraid, and skeptical about their ability to do this."

Board Selfies

Act on Passion

From time to time, we all get charged up, motivated, and committed. Perhaps the inspiration springs from a personal challenge. Or we witness an incident in the media. Our motivation lasts a moment, a day, a week, or a month. We fly high promising ourselves and others that we will act.

Then our motivation evaporates like a puddle after a rainstorm, shrinking hour by hour. We return to normal until the next cause awakens us. This time we feel less sure of our commitment, remembering our past failure to act.

You provide value by offering your members the opportunity to dismount the rollercoaster of good intentions. Board service delivers a path to match actions with passions.

The ability to take concrete action on your passion is one benefit of board service. You might already list this value when you recruit members. How, you wonder, does resource development work provide an even more significant advantage? It provides fuel for the cause and continuity of efforts, which otherwise would suffer from funding ups and downs.

Look at it this way: Board service enables one to move a cause forward a foot, board service that generates resources moves the cause forward a mile. Board members who help to obtain funds multiply their impact. Board service that produces revenue doubles, triples, and quadruples efforts compared to board service without revenue growth.

Here's an even more gratifying perspective. Imagine it,s five years from now. Your board members look back at their impact. They realize that they helped to create a sustainable, thriving, growing community and their satisfaction increases. By finding ways to put money in the nonprofit's bank account, they improve the world in a way that sticks.

Lastly, grand visions require collective actions. The need for collective action lies at the heart of why your founders established your nonprofit. Securing funding means you add resources to carry the cause forward. For instance, to get the Civil Rights Act of 1964 passed, Lyndon Johnson designed the process to convince Senator Everett Dirkson that he would be "a hero in history" if he supported the legislation. Likewise, board members who raise revenue become your organization's heroes forever.

Enhance Self-Esteem

Since money is frequently short in nonprofits, successfully acquiring funding enhances the self-worth of the procurer. Board members' self-esteem grows as they see themselves as people who get hard things done. Most people are afraid of fundraising, including your most respected and professional board members. Conquering fears, especially the fear of fundraising, provides a self-esteem boost. Plus, you helped them to overcome the fear of the unknown.

Gain Knowledge About Nonprofit Resource Development

Some years ago, as a member of the Association of Fundraising Professionals (AFP), I participated in a Youth in Philanthropy program. While the details of the program have grown hazy, the project included mentoring high school students about how to raise funds. The adult advisors helped the students pick a cause and develop a case. The ultimate experience was when I accompanied one teen on a call to an executive from a public utility company to ask for a gift for the cause. Before the meeting, the teen was all nerves and fears. After, she was thrilled, proud, and excited.

By taking similar actions, your board members will gain similar benefits plus personal knowledge about resource development to use the rest of their lives. In-the-trenches fundraising experiences generate in-depth knowledge, greater respect for the work, and more information than discussing possible actions around a board table.

Board Groupies

The benefits above encompass the personal gains your board members obtain when they engage in resource development. Participation also enhances how others view these individuals.

Enhance Brand and Create New Contacts

When board members engage in resource development, people see them as leaders who get things done. Participating in resource development also increases your members' contacts. For instance, your treasurer sits in on a grant site visit. During the meeting, he meets the head of the foundation. Later at a chamber meeting, your treasurer chats with this official and gets introduced to a new colleague. Subsequently, he closes some business with this new connection.

Achieve Amazing Things Together

Finally, never underestimate the value of asking someone to join with you to do something hard, because humans benefit from the struggle. Perhaps you remember this quote from John F. Kennedy.

"We choose to go to the Moon in this decade and do the other things, not because they are easy, but because they are hard, because that goal will serve to organize and measure the best of our energies and skills, because that challenge is one that we are willing to accept, one we are unwilling to postpone, and one which we intend to win…"

There are benefits to asking people to do something difficult. Nonprofits overlook them. If you can't imagine recruiting any member to help grow resources by telling them it will be hard, reexamine Kennedy's quote. It talks about making a choice and a reason why. The *why* is the opportunity to use our best skills and energies. Your board members gain when they do tough things like helping to raise money for your cause, since the task calls for working with others.

BRING IT HOME

QUESTIONS TO ASK BOARD MEMBERS TO FIND THE BEST ACTIVITIES TO DO TOGETHER

Why did you say yes? What might make you agree to serving again someday?

What would you like to achieve? How would you like to achieve it?

What do you love to do? If I call on you for advice, what would you enjoy working on with us?

A BIG, BOLD, UNDERLINED, AND ITALICIZED MESSAGE ABOUT GRATITUDE

Your board already does more for your organization than you or anyone knows. They talk about your good works to their families, peers, and friends. They ponder your efforts while driving to your meetings, in the shower, and as they go about their days. As they attend other events, they conjure ways the great ideas they encounter can benefit your organization. In the following pages, you're going to read about inviting your board to add new actions and behaviors to what they already do. Before doing so, I implore you to call out, celebrate, and express thanks for your board's current service.

Why? We know from reams of research that if you want more of a behavior (and you want more board help), you will get it by praising the smallest smidgen of the actions you seek. By affirming your board's current work leading your organization, you'll do more good for your efforts than if you adopt the familiar complaint that the board's not doing enough.

I'm not proposing that you run to your board and say "thank you" one time as a prelude to asking for help. Instead, appreciate what your board does and let them know it. Allow time for your gratitude to resonate. Specifically, if you include expressing gratitude as part of your next board meeting's agenda, do not follow up your recognition with a request for new help. That is, eliminate "thank you *and* ..." from your vocabulary and thinking. Why? New requests drown out and negate appreciation.

ADVANCED BOARD MEMBERS SKILLS

Do you recall Karen's Friends and Fortune Flowchart in chapter three? It includes six skills that support revenue growth. Those skills, you remember, can be practiced by anyone who wants to help your organization. Board members have additional opportunities. When your board takes on the following triplet of actions, they will accelerate your resource development and help you to raise millions together—sooner.

1. Make a Meaningful Stretch Gift

Board contributions are a must. Every member must give a cash donation once a year. You can tell your members I said so.

Stretch gifts invite your leadership to do more. These gifts demonstrate your board's leadership in concrete ways. They send a strong message. For one, they sing of good management. They proclaim that the board, from behind the closed doors of the nonprofit, likes what's happening. Stretch gifts announce that it's safe to invest in your organization. To anyone evaluating the risks of moving closer to your organization, stretch gifts shout safety.

What does making a meaningful, stretch gift mean? Every individuals determines what amount constitutes a stretch gift. What reflects a stretch for me may only be an annoyance fee for you, or vice versa.

Even though each board member independently determines what equals a stretch, universal criteria do apply. The following benchmarks will help your members to determine the amount that works for them. You might want to dog-ear this page so you can quickly return to it when you invite your board to make their next annual gift.

A stretch gift:

- is one of your top three philanthropic commitments this year;
- includes cash or assets that the nonprofit can turn into money (in-kind gifts are insufficient);
- is large enough to cause some unease, because the gift launches you into new philanthropic territory; and
- prompts a behavior change, such as giving up a daily coffee, skipping a splurge, or comparable budget impacts.

Here's a story that exemplifies the particulars of this final point. A board member privately approached me during a retreat. She was a pastor from a congregation that gives a major gift every year. Her leadership, in part, secures this gift. She shared that she also tithes and that finances at home are tight. Did she still need to give a stretch gift?

"Yes," I replied, "Here's why. Most foundations and thoughtful donors ask if 100 percent of the board gives a cash gift every year. A 'no' automatically disqualifies the nonprofit. More importantly, if even one board member doesn't give, it plants a seed of doubt in donors' minds. Donors wonder, 'What does *that* board member know that I don't know?'"

I returned to her situation, "You have special circumstances for not making a cash contribution or even a stretch gift. Unfortunately, nobody asks why board members aren't giving. People simply skip giving." We discussed how she might still make a gift. She decided that she would contribute unexpected cash, such as tax refunds, discounts, and money gifts she received for weddings and the like.

Beyond donations, in order to raise million together, offer your board members choices about how to help. The following two advanced board member skills will be beneficial to both them and the nonprofit. Invite your members to try both.

2. Discover People's Whys

We all have "philanthropic buttons." What is a philanthropic button? A philanthropic button is a reason or purpose you support specific causes. The issues behind our buttons explain why you got involved, why you stick with a cause, and why you continue to volunteer and donate.

Board members, because of their insider-outsider roles, stand in an excellent position to discover other people's buttons. Everyone has multiple buttons. When our buttons get pushed, we act.

Over time, each person cultivates unique buttons. Your buttons might spring from personal or family health issues, pets you had or wanted, or experiences you missed or enjoyed. Your buttons may have been formed when you were a child, adolescent, adult, or thirty minutes ago after listening to a newscast.

You can readily articulate some of your philanthropic passions. Others you will discover as you meet nonprofit leaders, consume media, and converse with friends. Surprisingly, you will identify some interests only after you write a check, attend an event, or otherwise actively support a nonprofit.

How can your board members help here? When your members practice this advanced skill, they ask people about their philanthropic interests. Why are board members ideal for this task? They're out circulating in the community and meeting people outside your Magic Circle of Next.

Once your board members identify people with philanthropic interest connected to your organizations, they share the contact information with staff and jointly decide on a follow-up plan.

Occasionally, the second step, creating a follow-up plan with staff, isn't necessary. For example, here at my desk, I'm looking at two-year-old Ali's picture of a daddy, mommy, and baby horse. As a Literacy Buddy with the Early Learning Coalition, each quarter I receive a sketch from a preschool child. My job as a volunteer is to send the child a book to read. I learned about the opportunity from Nick, the Coalition's board chair at a breakfast. This opportunity resonated with me because of my passion for books and interest in children. This program is an easy way to enter the organization. It provides a quarterly reminder to act on my philanthropic button.

3. Participate in the Full Development Process

To explain this third and final advanced board member skill, I begin by describing "the full development process." The total development process includes all the soft and hard skills of fundraising. That is, moving an individual from a stranger to an active donor in your nonprofit, giving a bequest or other major gift, and inviting others to join your community.

The process includes setting meetings, attending donor calls, making asks, participating in and taking on leadership in capital campaigns, and otherwise helping donors benefit from aligning with your organization. Board members who learn and participate in these tasks gain expertise. Since most board members serve multiple years, helping your board members participate in the whole process will offer your organization substantial returns.

Conclusion

"How do you grade your board in terms of helping you to obtain donated income?" I asked Andy Kramer, director of development at Southeastern Guide Dogs.

"100," he said. "If you aren't giving and getting, you have to wonder if you're in the wrong group." The organization's revenue growth supports Andy's testimony.

This chapter explored how nonprofits gain from board help in resource development, the many reasons board members benefit from helping nonprofits to grow revenue, and three skills where board members excel. For your board's benefit, invite your members to support revenue growth. You'd be remiss not to offer this great opportunity. Your offer will make them more effective as board members and more fulfilled human beings.

YOUR NOT-TO-DO TIP

LONG BOARD MEETINGS

Improve your board meetings by cutting your agenda in half. To achieve more, focus on the critical items. Over and over again, I find that one of the most useful skills for my clients is to reduce agendas. Pick your top points; save the rest for another time—or never (many issues resolve themselves).

CHAPTER SEVEN

STAFF CHAMPIONS: YOUR PAID SUPERHEROES

When Matthew Bisset, vice president for advancement at Eckerd College, began an $80 million capital campaign for new science facilities, he encountered skepticism from the science faculty. The staff didn't want to help, even though they'd benefit from the capital campaign that included science equipment they needed. With focused effort, the advancement department transformed the science department faculty into active fans. Over time, they became evangelists willing to travel and reach out to meet with and help donors. Eckerd's largest-ever campaign succeeded.

From caretakers to program managers, this chapter will help you to transform staff from bystanders to enthused participants in resource gathering. While Matthew's success involved professors, we explore all personnel, including full-time, part-time, and seasonal help. With their assistance, you'll be acing your revenue growth campaigns.

WHY DOES YOUR STAFF NEED TO HELP YOU DEVELOP RESOURCES?

Your staff already support your efforts to gather resources, but up until now, I'm guessing that you haven't recognized, inventoried, or fully celebrated their efforts. Nor, I speculate, have you capitalized on your staff's ability to grow your resources.

What can happen if you fail to organize your staff to help with resource development? Consider the experience of Duggan Cooley, the former executive director of Religious Community Services (RCS) and now head of the Community Foundation of Pinellas County.

"A fellow who might remind you of your grandfather drives up to the food bank in an old Cadillac," Duggan said. "He's neat and clean, but his clothing is frayed and worn."

The gentleman asked for a tour of the food bank.

"Sorry, no one's here right now who can do that."

The gentleman left and called RCS's main number and asked for the executive director from the parking lot. "I'd like to get a tour, but the folks here said no."

Duggan apologized and drove over to meet him. On the tour, the gentleman explained that he wanted to help hungry children. "Children shouldn't be hungry,'" the man said, clarifying his request for a tour. "This shouldn't be happening in this country."

He subsequently donated $50,000. Other gifts followed. Eventually, the man left RCS a bequest in his will.

RCS almost lost these valuable gifts. Imagine if the man hadn't called Duggan. Or if after the tour he remained so disillusioned by the initial encounter that he elected not to donate or to donate elsewhere. Could this happen at your organization?

Here are three critical lessons from the RCS experience:

- Opportunities to grow revenue surround nonprofits. You read about abundant resources in Chapter One. RCS's experience reminds you of this fact.

- Authorize your staff to say "yes" to reasonable request, that is, to use the Solve skill. Instead of catching opportunities, unempowered employees coax them out the door.

- Besides authorizing the staff, teach them to make helping people a priority. Duggan took advantage of the incident. He worked with staff to clarify the priority of serving people over completing warehouse tasks.

BRING IT HOME

START WITH SHOUT-OUTS

Take a minute to consider what's happening at your organization now regarding staff relationships to raising revenue.

What percentage of your staff help with income development?

How have your recognized or celebrated their involvement this quarter?

Which one of your employees can you thank at your next gathering? Jot their name in your calendar as a reminder to offer them a shout-out at your next meeting.

Why All Staff?

Numbers, Connections, Results

"Staff are often in the best position to know what people need. They're often great at building relationships and communicating because they're experts in their field. They tune in to what people need. They're often passionate and authentic. They make great spokespersons." — Judy Vredenburgh, president and CEO of Girls Inc.

Without staff engagement, nonprofits leave their soldiers at the office. Earlier, I estimated that each of your staff knows between two hundred and six hundred people. In the big picture, according to John Hopkins University Center for Civil Society Studies, nonprofit employment represents more than 10 percent of all United States jobs. The sector employs 10.7 million people. If every nonprofit employee directed just a smidgen of effort to growing revenue that resulted in $100 in new resources, the sector would be more than a billion dollars better off every year.

Besides staff size, why else is staff involvement imperative? Because they work with your donors, volunteers, and customers. Many staff members select nonprofit work because they have an affinity with your cause. With whom do they share this affinity? Your donors, volunteers, and customers. Many of these individuals cherish meaningful conversations with your staff around their shared passion. Staff interactions, both planned and spur of the moment, with people interested in your work, spark connections. Connections strengthen relationships.

Here's another way staff stands out. Employees can help your donors, customers, and volunteers to meet others using the Introduce skill. The more friendships a newcomer has with people in your community, the higher the likelihood that they will stay connected and become a fan.

Besides the irrefutable fact that your staff has the potential to enlarge your community and strengthen connections, what other reasons are there for staff to engage in income development?

- Staff enthusiasm inspires donors' confidence and contributions.

- Engaged staff, who understand the preciousness of resources, practice better stewardship.

Why do you want staff to help? It works. It's logical. Success requires it.

Why should staff want to help? Let's look at that now.

What's in It for Them?

Why Your Staff Will Want to Help Grow Your Resources

Why is it in your staff's best interest to join your efforts to increase the bottom line? Staff who help grow resources accrue benefits, including:

- enhanced job security
- greater comfort selling and marketing
- relationships with generous philanthropic people
- more resources for their work
- improved self-image
- excellent résumé content

How can you hire people open to helping you to develop resources? For some answers, consider the best practices of the Parkinson's Foundation.

BEST PRACTICES

WHOM TO HIRE

To enhance your ability to raise millions together, hire staff who have a connection with your cause, advises John Lehr, CEO of the Parkinson's Foundation. "Mission connections get expressed in many ways, such as participating in development, doing your job well, and husbanding resources."

When the foundation hires, they seek employees who want to help others, care about the cause, and are innately passionate. To augment these propensities, the foundation offers tools, skills, and knowledge. Besides using cross-functional teams, the foundation ensures that each staff member knows the organization's mission, values, and priorities. They also practice their elevator speeches.

You'll know you're hiring the right team when you experience low turnover, voluntary event participation, and staff-led challenges to raise funds, such as "Our department will raise more than your building." What other results might you expect from hiring well? In a recent year, the foundation received $7 million in legacy gifts from twenty donors. Staff projected 20 percent of the bequests; the rest John attributes to the foundation's culture of philanthropy.

How Can You Do That?

Seek employees that:

1. connect to your cause

2. express enthusiasm

3. get jazzed up by the chance to change the world

Give them:

1. skills, tools, and knowledge

2. a deep understanding of your mission and your values

3. practice giving elevator pitches

Ask them to:

1. do their job well

2. participate in development

3. husband resources

Staff and Donor Magic

As members of the Nature Conservancy Legacy Club, my husband and I attended an event at the Tiger Creek Preserve in Florida. After a brief welcome from the development staff and a promise to be back by 11:30 a.m., the program team took over. We climbed aboard a swamp buggy to tour the five-thousand–acre preserve. At stops along the way, we wandered trails as the staff pointed out their work and fauna, including a swallow-tailed kite.

Ninety minutes into the tour, we were late for our box lunch at headquarters. As the hour approached noon, a development staff member interrupted our questions and acknowledged they had broken their word. They offered anyone who wanted to go back for lunch a second buggy.

No one moved. Why? We craved more time with the staff. Someone asked a question, and we continued our learning fest.

 IMPORTANT

ALL STAFF ON BOARD

This means *everyone helps*.

Not everyone does the same thing.

All of your staff won't provide tours for major donors, but almost every major donor would be interested in learning about the work of individuals and what the donations did or will do for your cause. Some of your staff's value lies in their knowledge. By sharing their expertise, they can help donors and customers experience your organization in meaningful ways. In the next section, you'll explore the overall process of staff resource-gathering skill development.

THE STAFF DEVELOPMENT PROCESS

IMPORTANT

WITH AND WITHOUT

"Without a flourishing staff, you'll never have a flourishing organization." —Val Wright, president, Val Wright Consulting

Moving from "I Hate Fundraising" to a Culture of Resource Development

Remember your first swim class? After lots of splashing, your instructor got your attention and invited everyone to use the water to get his or her face wet. Likewise, staff begins helping to raise resources excited, fearful, and with modest requests.

What processes can you use to help your staff to develop resources? Start by noticing how your team contributes now. Affirm these actions. From here, help them move from being beginners to intermediates, and finally to resource development swimmers with a series of steps.

Level One: Beginner Skills

Let's get specific. What can your humble watch person, and any other staff member who has little role in providing the mission, do to increase your resources? Several practical activities. He or she can decide to view interruptions to work as opportunities to kindle relationships with supporters. He or she can greet visitors, graciously accept correspondence, deliver information, and answer basic questions such as "Can I park here?" The beginning stages of building a culture of philanthropy share common ground with high-quality customer service.

To give you a better understanding of beginner actions that support resource development, I turn back to Hosting, the first skill in Karen's Friends and Fortune Flowchart.

Beginner Skill Example: Hosting

The medical office was dark and gloomy. At the front desk, the staff responded but failed to look at me. During my forty-five-minute wait, I saw one smile—and that was from someone in scrubs from another office. I vowed never to return.

Likewise, donors don't want to deepen relationships in settings of dismal gloom. Creating a warm welcome supports resource development. All staff can welcome visitors. Julie, for instance, greets a guest, offers assistance, and when the guest needs help finding an office, accompanies her to it.

Action: Ask your staff to act as hosts during working hours and whenever they attend community events. They adopt the host role even if the event's *not* your event.

Most of your staff will readily understand the logic of greeting visitors and using the flowchart skills. However, some may be unclear about *exactly* what you want them to say and do. When I work with leaders, I often find that when they ask others to perform a task they know well, they offer vague instructions. They mesh steps together. Without details, listeners use their judgment. They end up with results that are creative but not in a good way. To obtain quality results, err on the side of overly detailed instruction.

Here's my advice about the details. List tasks in sequential action. For example, by hosting, you:

- notice a newcomer
- approach them
- make eye contact
- smile
- speak
- offer your help

And, the person must decide which, if not all, of the above steps are appropriate in the setting.

Beginner Skill Example: Giving

Leaders often hesitate to ask their staff for donations. After all, your staff *already* does so much. You fret that you can't pay them what they're worth. So you don't ask.

If this is you, you've forgotten the joy of giving and the benefits your staff will gain by contributing. Asking staff to donate offers everyone the opportunity to enjoy the benefits of philanthropy, including greater happiness and understanding why donors give.

On a practical level, how can you do this with appeal? Here's a best practice from the Girl Scouts of Greater Atlanta. These scouts invite their staff to be part of their $1,000-a-year Giving Circle. When staff joins a circle, they attend Giving Circle events as honored guests. That is, they *don't* work the event.

Here's another possibility: What if you replaced your annual holiday gift exchange with a gift to the organization in honor of another team member's work?

Action: Establish an expectation that 100 percent of your staff members give to your nonprofit once a year. Make the amount private. The only other guideline is that they can't give the gift for their personal benefit. In other words, a staff member can give to a similar program in a branch across the city, but not to their office. One study found that when team members gave fifteen euros to other team members, it generated seventy-nine euros of organizational benefit.

 ## BRING IT HOME

HOW TO CRAFT OTHER BEGINNER OPPORTUNITIES

To raise millions together, you'll want to design more beginner opportunities. What do beginner resource developers need?

1. Encouragement and safety, such as a safe place to practice new skills and a chance to express fears.

2. Specific instructions about tasks, including steps, phrases to use, and plans for contingencies, especially for contingencies that involve their worst fears.

3. Recognition for following through, no matter if the results are positive, neutral, or even detrimental. Beginners thrive on praise for trying.

Level Two: Intermediate Skills

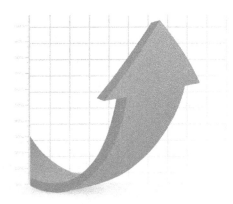

An invisible divider splits beginner and intermediate staff philanthropic evangelists. On the beginner side, staff engages in resource development to meet job expectations. On the intermediate margin, they participate because they see personal and professional benefits.

What Do Intermediates Need?

At this level, staff discusses resource development issues. You start to see a return on their efforts. Your culture's changing for the good. With the pressure of other duties and needs, you'll be tempted to move on to other tasks. Don't! Unless you want to start all over again, keep your expectation of staff engagement in resource development front and center.

Intermediates need skill growth, encouragement, and a sense of permanence. Luckily, you can support all three with one stroke. How so? Keep income development front and center in your priorities and conversations. That is, no matter what happens, staff involvement in resource growth remains permanently on the agenda. Otherwise, people will assume that resource development is just another trend that will soon be replaced by a new fad. Without your continued focus, things will revert to their old normal, except you will see more cynicism growing in your backyard.

Here's one way to keep the focus high without becoming burdensome: Conduct weekly fifteen-minute resource development check-ins. At them, confirm if your income development goals are still relevant. Then ask each staff member to share what they accomplished the past week. Recognize the accomplishments and ask about their intentions for the next week. Then send them on their way. Your expectation of action and public reporting will prevent your resource development initiative from joining past change efforts lost in the dust heap of good intentions.

Intermediates need encouragement. They benefit from praise and the opportunity to enjoy their successes—just like donors who see that their efforts make a difference. You help by crafting expectations, praising accomplishments, and showing them how their efforts help the organization.

One staff member at the Boys & Girls Clubs of Metro Atlanta, is an excellent example of an intermediate's journey. During her thirty-year tenure at the organization, the staff member gathered many in-kind gifts. She wanted, however, nothing to do with fundraising. When the Facebook fan page fad began, her coworkers knew this employee needed to make a fan page. Giving in to peer pressure, she created a page that generated $5,000. Who on your staff needs encouragement, permission to try something new, or just a nudge?

Next, you'll read about two intermediate actions that support resource development. The first comes from Speaks in Karen's Friends and Fortune Flowchart. The second will spring from your weekly check-ins.

At the intermediate level, you place less emphasis on specific steps. Instead, share your goals. Then jointly explore the options on the best ways to move toward them. As the leader, contribute and listen to the ideas. When you see the best approach, direct your staff to move forward on it.

Intermediate Skill Example: Speaks

Amplify Media

Besides creating a fan page, intermediate staff can help your organization to amplify your marketing. Staff at this level can magnify your organization's voice in the market. It's like turning up the volume button on your car's speakers.

To illustrate this concept, here are two options, one for electronic communications and a second for print media.

1. *Electronic Communications.* Ask employees to forward your event announcements to friends and relatives via email, text, and the like. Also, request staff to like your posts and, more importantly, to comment on them.

2. *Print Communications.* In your meeting room, place stamps, envelopes, address labels, and flyers for upcoming events. Ask staff to send the announcement with a personal note to friends and contacts from your mailing lists with whom they have a relationship.

Action: Brainstorm with staff ways your personnel can boost your media presence. Pick the top ideas. Measure your results. Include the number of people you reached with a personal touch.

Intermediate Skill Example: Determine the Best Way to Obtain Results

Intermediates can share about how best to support your organization's revenue growth. By listening to their peers, they'll discover new ideas on how to get results. Your staff might think they don't like fundraising, but as they experience success, they'll learn that fundraising includes many diverse activities, some of which they enjoy.

Action: As you gather staff, ask to hear both their joys and challenges about raising resources. Ask what they would do again and what they wouldn't repeat.

Level Three: Swimmer Skills

A second invisible divide exists between intermediates and swimmers. On the intermediate side, staff members think, *I support resource development because it's good for my career*. On the swimmer side, they think, *I help because it's good for me, the organization, and the donors*.

What Do Swimmers Need?

For swimmers, resource development has become part of what they do. To continue to swim, swimmers need opportunities to participate and receive kudos for exemplary results.

For example, musicians at the Florida Orchestra participate in fundraising in two ways. First, they join calls to donors. Musicians enjoy the experience. Why? The conversations focus on music, something everyone in the room loves.

Musicians can also agree to be sponsored in the orchestra's sponsor-a-musician program. "It's surprising how little this program requires," shares Michael Pastreich, former president and CEO of the Florida Orchestra. "While some sponsors pick a musician to sponsor, usually staff suggests a musician based on mutual interests."

In exchange for their $10,000 donation, the sponsors and sponsored musician enjoy a meal together. During the year, the musician attends any special event that the sponsor attends. The result? A variety of relationships. One musician–sponsor relationship deepened to include sharing a weekly Shabbat meal. Another involves exchanges of friendly greetings. Most partners establish a connection somewhere between these two extremes.

Finally, the orchestra enjoys enhanced revenue year to year. Many sponsors renew.

Besides the example of the Florida Orchestra's musicians, this chapter shared examples of swimmer staff at Eckerd College, the Parkinson's Foundation, and the Nature Conservancy. In short, swimmers help with the task you put in front of them.

 BRING IT HOME

ALL HANDS ON DECK

On the first day of swim class, everyone gets tested. Likewise, rank your staff members. When it comes to resource development, who is a beginner, intermediate, and swimmer? What support do they need to function at their best? Make a plan.

YOUR NOT-TO-DO TIP

ALL TOGETHER NOW FOR FIFTEEN MINUTES OR LESS

Substitute long staff meetings with fifteen-minute check-ins. Consider standing for the duration. Your agenda includes three items:

- Do our goals still make sense?
- What happened since we last met, including joys and challenges?
- What will you do before we meet next week?

CHAPTER EIGHT

SPECIAL STAFF CASE: CEOS, DEVELOPMENT, AND DONATED INCOME

"I just wish that he would stop having such long lunches and raise some money" --overheard from a CEO, speaking about a well-respected major gift officer.

To grow revenue, contrary to wisdom on Nonprofit Street, the most critical relationship is not the one between the donor and their nonprofit contact. It's the one between the CEO and the chief of development (COD). This chapter zeroes in on donated income, this relationship, and the magic and hard work that make CEO and development staff relationships fruitful. You'll read about the challenges inherent in this liaison, including coordinating efforts, generating mutual expectations, measuring success, dealing with the capricious timing of revenue, and high development staff turnover.

 BEST PRACTICES

A TALE OF FOUR LETTERS

Before RozeLyn Beck started her job as the vice president of philanthropy and development for the Commemorative Air Force, the organization conducted a donor wealth screening. Wealth-screening tools help to determine donors' capacities to give.

The organization discovered that no one in their Dallas headquarters knew the highest net-worth couple in the database. The couple had been members for forty years and donated periodically, from $200 to $10,000. The screening revealed that they had made several multimillion dollar gifts to colleges and universities. Due to staff turnover, they weren't on anyone's radar.

Letter One. The CEO wrote a communication to the couple. The correspondence introduced the CEO, apologized for not reaching out earlier, and stated that the CEO would like to meet them.

Letter Two. A few weeks later, the Commemorative Air Force received a reply. The prospects were frequently in Dallas. They'd stop by the next time they were in town and would send dates soon.

Letter Three. The donor sent a letter with some proposed meeting times. On the arranged date, the couple met with the CEO and RozeLyn. During the conversation, the CEO raised the possibility of a major gift. The prospects responded positively and promised to consider the request.

Letter Four. Within a week, a letter arrived from the couple. It contained a $1 million pledge.

Let's unpack this story. It contains four insights to help you grow revenue.

1. There are treasures in your backyard. If your organization has long-time members who give, even erratically, you have prospects for major and planned gifts, including bequests.

2. If you don't ask for help, you won't get it. Do any people in your database believe you don't need their financial assistance?

3. Occasionally, your fundraising will be easy and straightforward, like this Commemorative Air Force experience. Mostly it won't. After closing this gift, RozeLyn's new challenge became helping her board and boss to understand that while they *might* discover similar treasures in their backyard, it wasn't likely.

4. Two heads are better than one. The CEO and RozeLyn worked together to close this gift, including drafting the letter, planning the meeting, and handling the pledge.

Development experts, including your development staff, help organizations to sort priorities, find contacts, organize efforts, and create processes. Additionally, CEOs frequently direct development staff to arrange and lead the organization's philanthropic education so that everyone gains the skills they need to help grow resources.

Raising millions together requires coordination between the CEO and development staff. At the very least, this requires that the CEO protect development staff so they can work. This means that the CEO doesn't actively undermine their efforts by complaining about how many long lunches they take, assigning other tasks, and so forth. Even if the CEO only protects the development staff so they can focus on building relationships, it helps.

If the CEO refuses to lead the development staff or let them access the board, development staff members can still embark upon resource-gathering efforts, but their efforts will be limited to donors, vendors, and others with whom they can establish relationships. The bulk of the organization's power—that is, staff and board resource development—will operate at half throttle, at best.

Benefits for CEO

"Good development staff takes a solid vision cast by the CEO and helps the organization hone it and translate it into stories. The plot of these stories is how donors help and partner to make the vision come true." — Ann Logan, vice president of development, Marie Selby Botanical Gardens

Ann Logan's words point out the ultimate CEO benefit of working well with the development staff: the CEO gets to fulfill his or her vision. While not every CEO takes their role with the hope that their work will make a difference, most CEOs do. For many, the position offers them the opportunity to apply a lifetime of insights, skills, and wisdom.

In high functioning CEO–development staff relationships, CEOs pass on the vision to the staff. The development staff catches the vision like a good contagion. Development personnel think about all the donors in the database and match the CEO's vision to potential donors. From here, they share the vision with individual donors and help them to catch its magic and fund it.

Successfully executing your vision is one of the benefits CEOs gain by turbocharging their work with their development staff. CEOs who develop remarkable relationships with these staff members also improve the way they manage the organization. Why? Greater direct involvement with development reduces the mystery of fundraising. CEOs become better able to measure the effectiveness of the work and grow it.

Traditionally, fundraising gets placed in a silo that requires CEOs to monitor development personnel, who, at best, spend little time in the office. They are out doing hard-to-measure activities. They're off having long lunches, schmoozing at other nonprofits' events, and meeting prospects for a round of golf. How can the CEO know if these are the *right* lunches, golf partners, and events? More importantly, how will the CEO know if different relationships are ripe to request a major gift? Without involvement, the CEO relies on the development personnel's discernment.

What's even more challenging for CEOs is the fact that since most major gifts take several years to close, the return on the investment made in development staff tends to be erratic. When dollars fail to flow in early in a development staff's tenure, CEOs worry about the budget drain and might tune into the discontent of other CEOs with their development staff. They hear about high development staff turnover.

All this changes when the CEO shifts development to a central organizational function. When it comes to replacing or adding development staff, the CEO using the Let's Raise Nonprofit Millions Together approach enjoys a much greater appreciation of the talents needed. Not only is the CEO more aware of the development process, but they are also better able to measure the success of staff, affirm it, identify needed improvements, and direct resources. Finally, the CEO contributes to the discernment process of whom to ask, what to do, and when to ask providing improved decisions.

There are strong incentives for CEOs to work well with their development staff. Incentives include obtaining their vision, easing management concerns about development, and growing resources.

Benefits of the Let's Raise Nonprofit Millions Together Approach for Development Personnel

Being a director of development with a traditional development approach can be exhausting. Besides identifying donors, forming relationships, maintaining records, and growing a community of support, you often need to deal with insiders who don't understand how development works—some of whom snipe at you. Others, like board members, wonder when you'll *show them the money!* You perpetually feel one large donation away from job security.

Trying to convince people that there is no magic makes the work harder. Leadership thinking goes like this, "If we hire the right staff member we will access their Rolodex and, in time, the donors they know." The Let's Raise Nonprofit Millions Together process crushes this approach because everyone begins to think about donations from the donor's perspective. With this approach, development directors face fewer demands for miracles and more requests for relationship-building help. The results offer better job security and outcomes.

When an organization commits to engaging everyone in raising resources, the development staff's role shifts. Their new functions include the opportunity to reach more donors and teach more philanthropy. Begging and cajoling transform into inviting, affirming, and challenging peers, board members, donors, and others to practice new skills. Instead of being perceived as nags, development staff members become coaches of learners. They coordinate resource development. While development staff remain vigilant about what's on the scoreboard, they lead a team putting balls into baskets, instead of just playing themselves.

By teaching others the mechanism of resource development, development directors fine-tune their fundraising skills. They prove the maxim that if you want to learn something—teach it. They break down activities from automatic processes into concrete steps for others to duplicate. It's a bit like teaching basketball. When is it time to dribble? When is it best to pass? When is it time to make a shot? Although development's still about scoring, you have a heck of a lot more help getting the ball near the net and taking shots. Over time, development gets more exciting, interesting, and profitable.

Imagine it's five years down the road and your board, staff, vendors, donors, and volunteers each bring the name of one prospect per month to your organization. As development director, you now have an enviable time management challenge. You'll have too many avenues to pursue.

This is good news. Lots of prospects stretch the odds of over-the-threshold gifts that is, people who give to you with no or little solicitation. Secondly, more donors mean that you can afford to provide people time to respond since you're off meeting other prospects. Finally, large donor bases allow you to divide your donors and treat each segment differently. Animal nonprofits, for instance, increase revenue by segmenting donors into cat lovers and dog lovers and sending different requests to each.

For development personnel, the benefits of the Let's Raise Nonprofit Millions Together mindset include increased job security, more help, and more satisfying work. To illustrate what this skill-building looks like from the development perspective, I'd like to introduce you to Jennifer Darling.

BEST PRACTICES

THE EDUCATION OF A DEVELOPMENT DIRECTOR

When the Denver Art Museum conducted its capital campaign, Jennifer Darling was the director of development and membership. The campaign incorporated multiple chairs to fulfill the museum's and volunteers' needs.

One chair was a successful businessman. People considered the man difficult. "People were scared of him," said Jennifer, now vice president of philanthropy at Children's Hospital Colorado. "He also succeeded at whatever he decided to do."

Working with this tough chair challenged Jennifer to do her best. To meet his needs, she super-prepared for meetings. "His stubbornness to succeed brought out my stubbornness to help him meet his goal."

A second chair was extremely social. This chair was always contacting Jennifer to ask for nice extras, such as sending birthday cards or notes congratulating a donor whose child got into West Point. From this chair, Jennifer learned new methods to grow relationships and cheer others on to victory.

The multiple chairs helped Jennifer to gain confidence. The campaign succeeded in raising funds to double their building space and earned $12 million.

How Can You Do That?

Adapt your style to the style of your volunteers. Each of Jennifer's cochairs, for instance, preferred different communication frequencies. Some wanted to hear from her once a week. Others sought daily updates.

Do whatever it takes to help your volunteers thrive. Regularly ask: "How can I help you to succeed?"

As you teach philanthropy, learn from others. Discover how they operate. Value it, particularly when the style differs from your preferences. Remember that your organization asks individuals to lead because these individuals know how to succeed. Since many paths lead to success, discover new routes.

Jennifer's lessons point us to the value of trust in relationships. Because Jennifer adapted her style to fit her volunteers' needs, they learned to trust her. The next section explores trust between the CEO and the development staff. It begins with another true story.

TRUST AND THE CEO–DEVELOPMENT RELATIONSHIP

In a quiet corner in a city's most elegant restaurant, a couple declines a naming opportunity. When the new CEO realizes what is happening, he blurts into the suddenly silent room, "You're not going to fund it!" The chief of development kicks him under the table.

Despite this unfortunate start, over time, this relationship between CEO and COD succeeds. They receive a substantial gift from the couple and millions for their nonprofit from other donors.

Unfortunately, too few CEO and development relationships reach their potential. When this partnership flounders, nonprofits pay twice. First, they waste salary dollars. Second, they lose donations. CompassPoint's 2013 study *Underdeveloped: A National Study of Challenges Facing Nonprofit Fundraising* found "high levels of instability and uncertainty in the development director position." These include "high turnover, long vacancies, and performance problems." *Underdeveloped* confirmed what many experts in the nonprofit field already know. "The relationship is not easily managed," explains Ann Decker, executive director of the Indian River State College Foundation.

Can more nonprofits benefit from healthier relationships between their CEO and development chiefs? As part of my consulting work, I conducted a series of interviews with and about successful CEO–development teams. These discussions lead me to develop the Trust Pyramid. The information from the conversations and the pyramid will help strengthen your CEO–development partnership.

Trust: The Foundation of Success

What makes CEO–development relationships work? Trust. To help you to better understand successful CEO–development relationships, the Trust Pyramid divides trust into four components. You start at the bottom of the pyramid, and, as trust grows, you move upward.

Level One: Strong Ethics

"The first nonprofit I served received a bequest earmarked to reduce debt. The CEO asked the board's permission to use the funds for a new building. It was, he advised, an expedient way to launch the capital campaign. In my mental time machine, I've often returned to that meeting to speak for the deceased donor and insist that we use the funds for debt reduction." —Anonymous

The ethics of the CEO and the COD form the foundation of their relationship. To establish trust, the individual ethics of each person must be strong. According to Peg Lowery, retired executive director of the State College of Florida Foundation, each person in the relationship must be a "quality human being." Moreover, to raise significant individual donations, both partners need strong ethics around fundraising. Why are strong ethics so fundamental?

Strong Ethics Protect the Organization. The greater a nonprofit's success, the more likely it will meet donors, knowingly or not, who seek to use the nonprofit for their gain. Research demonstrates that people will cheat more for a cause than for their own benefit.

Strong Ethics Simplify Life. Before a meeting, a CEO accidentally dents a donor's car. When the donor notices the damage, the CEO denies causing it, despite the visible matching red paint on the CEO's car. The COD apologizes, pays for the repair with her funds, and shortly takes a new position.

Strong Ethics Support Donor Confidence. Like people everywhere, astute donors know more than they consciously process. When they sense ethical quicksand, they depart for other shores.

Strong Ethics Support Long-term Relationships. Jan Pullen, head of school at Saint Stephen's Episcopal School in Bradenton, Florida, said their motto, "We do what we say," inspires donors. Gary W. Cain, president and chief professional officer with the Boys & Girls Clubs of Central Florida, shares, "Most donors' entry points are not one million dollars. Instead, major gifts are a long and slow process over the years."

Level Two: Confidence in Each Other's Competence

Strong ethics form the foundation of a trusting CEO–COD relationship. For these relationships to reach their potential, trust must grow. Successful relationships require each partner's belief that the other is competent to do his or her job. "I've hired development directors that look good on paper, but lacked the talent set to succeed," said Thom Stork, former president/CEO of the Florida Aquarium. Often, trust must be given before the results manifest. Outcomes, such as funds raised and promises fulfilled, strengthen belief in others' competence.

For the CEO, belief in the COD's competence starts with respecting fundraising as a professional endeavor. If the CEO undervalues fundraising, it is likely he or she will also undervalue the individuals engaged in the profession.

Development staff who believe in their CEO's competency confidently tell donors, "You can count on us." CODs rely on their CEO's competence to create donor trust that funded projects will get done.

Level Three: Realistic Expectations

Two people with strong ethics and belief in each other's competence can still lack trust. CEO and COD create the third level of trust by agreeing on the overall process of how to obtain individual donations. In this level of trust, the CEO and COD agree on three essentials:

1. *Starting Point.* Are we ready to raise significant donor funds, or do we need to do more work? Does our culture need to shift? Some organizations need tweaks, others serious overhauls.

2. *Roles.* What role will the CEO play? What roles will the staff and board play? If they will play a role, how will we organize it?

3. *Measurement.* How will we know we are making progress? How long will this take?

Trust requires agreement between the CEO and development staff about how fundraising works and what needs to happen next. You build successful relationships by meeting regularly and setting clear expectations and accountability. You create trust when each partner communicates a mutual understanding of the goals and the process to obtain them.

Level Four: Teamwork

"Our planned ask for one donor was $10,000," shared Mark Haney, former vice president of advancement at the Florida Aquarium. "In the meeting, the donor mentioned that she had just given $150,000 to an organization she liked just as much as the aquarium. So I went off script and asked for $100,000. Thom [the president/CEO] followed my lead, even though we planned for him to make the ask. We closed a $50,000 gift."

The correction Mark and Thom made mid-meeting represents both great collaboration and the fourth level of trust: teamwork. As members of a team, both the CEO and COD accept responsibility for outcomes, money or no.

"CEOs are actively engaged in the relationship-building process. They also maintain a regular dialogue with their COD, sharing goals and supporting mutual strategies," said Julie Britton, vice president of development at Straz Center for the Performing Arts.

Team play allows each partner to work wholeheartedly toward success because any success *is* their success. Since donor meetings always require improvisation, collaboration shines here and provides high dividends.

The combination of strong ethics, belief in the other's competence, shared expectations, and team play creates a successful fundraising environment. When all four levels of trust are present, donors, the CEO, the COD, and the organization benefit.

BRING IT HOME

USE THE TRUST PYRAMID AS A DIAGNOSTIC

How can you use the Trust Pyramid to diagnoses your CEO and development director relationship? Consider these questions:

- Do you share common ethics around fundraising issues?
- In what ways does your partner show they respect your competence?
- Do you regard fundraising as a profession?
- Where do you agree and disagree on the process needed to raise funds?
- In what ways do you engage as a team for fundraising?

If you find you have a healthy relationship, explore where you can improve it. If you discover shaky trust, identify the cause and, with that knowledge, build a solution.

HIRING

"It takes three years of work for a development director even to make a good start." —Craig Badinger, the Hermitage Artist Retreat

Even though many significant donor relationships take years to form, development staff turnover remains high. The next section looks at tasks and characteristics to consider as you interview development candidates.

How to Hire Exceptional Development Staff

Imagine you're hiring a new development staff member. You sit at your desk flipping through a stack of candidate emails. Your first task is to discern who to interview.

162

The Written Word

To help, here's some wisdom springing from a conversation I had with Matthew Bissett, vice president for advancement at Eckerd College. Evaluate written materials, such as resumes and email letters, to see if they demonstrate suitable writing and development skills.

Review the cover letter. Does it contain a large number of ego strokes for the writer? If so, pass on the applicant. While positive self-esteem is a must, avoid egomaniacs. Successful development specialists pull people together for the common good. It's the cause and case that generate donations, not individuals.

Is the letter customized? Did the writer write to an individual or a mailbox? Did they create a personalized case for an interview? Customization suggests they will treat donors as unique.

Moreover, did the candidate show you how you're connected? Links might mention that you once met, went to the same college, once vacationed in your state, and so forth. Since the individual you will hire will meet many new people, sharing a link in their letter suggests that the person understands how to kindle relationships.

Finally, does the material contain proper grammar? Do they use short paragraphs that match our Twitter-like attention spans? Do the words convey warmth without too much ease? If you hire the applicant, he or she will represent your organization. Will they do a worthy job?

This evaluation, along with a review of different backgrounds and experiences will help you to reduce your pool of candidates to a reasonable number. Now it's time to conduct interviews.

Interviews

If you still have lots of candidates, begin with telephone interviews. The telephone, like the letter, is an essential development tool.

Listen to how different candidates answer your questions and to the questions they ask. How do their telephone skills compare to other candidates?

During interviews, both on the phone and in person, seek answers to these questions:

- How many small gifts from new donors did the person obtain last year? (Small gifts tend to reflect the work of individuals. Major gifts necessitate teamwork.)

- What evidence does the person offer of being a self-starter?

- What indications does the candidate give of employing a collective approach to raising funds?

- Does the individual match the style of the person to whom they are speaking? (Yes, more than one person should interview your top candidates.)

- Is the candidate vetting your organization? (Good candidates want to understand the challenges they'll face and seek a good fit too.)

- Does the conversation conclude with a next step-that is, a mini-contract about who will do what next and the timeline? (This contract improves your confidence in the candidate's ability to move donor relationships forward.)

Now that I've outlined a best practice development candidate process ,let's turn to the task of hiring a CEO who supports development efforts and the teamwork behind the Let's Raise Nonprofit Millions Together process. I focus on hiring an executive without a fundraising background.

Hiring the Never-Been-in-Development CEO

If your organization depends on growing donated income, you'll want to hire chief executives with the skills or willingness to lead development efforts. What attitudes, skills, and mindsets do these executives need?

Seek candidates who:

- cast an inspiring vision you get excited about creating with them;
- verbalize that fundraising benefits organizations and donors;
- express comfort letting the development staff work with the board to educate them and encourage their philanthropy;
- provide references from development personnel who verify that the candidate actively engaged in resource development;
- state a willingness to meet with major donors and ask for donations, since you can't say "I won't fundraise-" at the same time you ask others to do so; and
- convey confidence in their ability to raise funds with the help of the board, staff, and others, demonstrating a collective approach.

When you hire development staff, the critical asset you seek is the ability to raise funds. When you hire an executive director, raising funds, while vital, is not the only skill you need. The criteria above will help you in hiring a CEO who will lead the charge of raising millions together.

This chapter explored the most critical relationship in donated income: between the CEO and the individual responsible for development. When the people filling the two roles build a partnership based on trust, they will steer your whole organization to doubling, tripling, and, even quadrupling the donated funds you raise.

RECYCLING DEVELOPMENT STAFF

If your organization has hired a series of development directors whose tenures average less than three years, stop. Before you hire a new staff member, examine your organization to find out why. Rapid, repeat turnovers that take place in three years or less point to challenges inside organizations, *not* in the employees. Here are several areas where I've seen the most challenges:

Hiring

It's easy to get dazzled by recent major gifts made to the candidate's current employer. Organizations grow dreamy-eyed thinking about how the person will bring their movers-and-shakers list to a new nonprofit. (This only happens when donors seek the new connection.) Don't be swayed by what a team accomplished unless you hire the whole team and start in a similar place. Instead, focus on how many *new* donors the candidate secured during their tenure.

Unrealistic Expectations

Unless you start at less than $20,000 in donated income per year, without other changes, you should not expect that hiring a new development staff person will increase contributed revenue by 50 percent in year one. Extend this expectation to three years to be more realistic.

Infrastructure Needs

Each development team member needs approximately two hundred prospects or current donors with whom to engage when they start a position. This number roughly translates to one appointment per working day for a year. Even though you and the new employee will add donors during the year, too many organizations hire development staff without an adequate pool of prospective donors in place. Before you add development staff, build your community first.

Use these tips to stop recycling development staff to save time and raise more resources.

CHAPTER NINE

TREASURES IN YOUR BACKYARD: RAISING MILLIONS WITH VOLUNTEERS, CUSTOMERS, AND DONORS

True story.

The phone rang. Tracy, the development director at the opera, answered.

A donor was calling. "I just met someone who would *be perfect* for us," she said. "I'm bringing them to the first performance of the season. I'll pay for their seats, but can you arrange for us to sit together? And, will you meet them during intermission?"

Tracy was thrilled with this request and the consequences. Within a year, the couple donated $50,000.

The Let's Raise Nonprofit Millions Together opportunity doesn't end with the board and staff; that is, folks you pay or who agree to serve. The approach, exemplified by the opera donor, demonstrates that the interests and energy of donors, customers, and volunteers can be harnessed to support your resource development. Some of your most exciting revenue will spring from these individuals. This chapter highlights these opportunities and helps you to increase volunteers, customers, and donors who help you to raise millions together.

Not Accidents

Donors, customers, and volunteers who value your organization don't see themselves as outsiders. They consider your organization their organization. In a sense, they have melded their minds with your efforts and the cause.

When did this start? Sometimes these individuals have a long history with the organization that predates current staff. Others adopted your organization the moment they stepped into your doors. Most deep connections happen over time as they become your regulars.

How did the sense of ownership happen? They responded to your requests. They fortuitously got engaged when a friend invited them. They hung around, accepting invitations to attend events and to help. They saw your needs and wanted results. Over time, they became committed to your work.

Why do they help? Why did the opera donor invite friends and reach out to the development director for assistance? Your donors, volunteers, and customers realize that your nonprofit needs revenue. They might want to help your cause. Alternatively, they might want to enhance their relationships by having more fun at your events by inviting their friends. While they may have mixed motivations—and who does not—they help. They can, with your support, do more and become your organization's extended eyes, ears, and hands. They can connect you to people in your Magic Circle of Next.

Up until now, volunteers, donors, and customers who help have been an uncelebrated and often untapped lifeline to nonprofit resources. What's exciting about them? Most folks don't include these individuals as part of their team. By recognizing their value, you'll be able to both celebrate and support their efforts and help them to produce more results.

YOUR VOLUNTEER, CUSTOMER, AND DONOR ASSETS

Before I explore how to work with volunteers, customers, and donors, let's define these subgroups.

Volunteers. By volunteers, of course, I mean people who give their time. Traditionally, volunteers serve on committees, help at the front desk, and read to children in your childcare center. Long-term volunteers are your best bet for resource development help.

Donors. Donors give money. Focus your efforts on current donors who give regularly. Also, prioritize individuals who indicate to you that they made a bequest to your organization. In other words, seek donors who demonstrate long-term commitment.

Customers. Customers include people who buy products and services from you. They comprise your clients, people who purchase event tickets, or rent your housing units for their child with special needs. Your best prospects are repeat customers who have used your services for years.

Let's explore why you'll find these three groups so helpful to your work to grow millions together.

Why You Need Them

Good Words

A friend just texted me to ask where I bought the almond butter I mentioned. More than GuideStar, Amazon, or other review services, we seek and follow the advice of relatives, friends, and neighbors. "The most credible form of advertising comes straight from the people we know and trust," states an article on the Nielsen Global Trust website.

During a strategic planning meeting, Betty, a substantial donor and a board member, added to my explanation of how the board could impact the organization's revenue with this testimonial: "I tell my friends that if they give, the names of their loved ones can be on a building *forever.*"

Giving recommendations and referrals is just one way our volunteers, customers, and donors help. Even by casually talking about donating to you or using your services or product, they enhance your brand. You benefit when your volunteers, customers, and donors share kind words about you. In some cases, you gain new customers and donors.

They Expand Your Magic Circle of Next with People Perfect for You

When volunteers, customers, and donors talk about you to their acquaintances, they touch your Magic Circle of Next. As unpaid spokespersons (in the case of volunteers), and even people who pay (in the case of donors and customers), their actions speak convincingly in the busy marketplace.

Not only do these voices get heard, but the right people hear the sounds. Remember the cliché "birds of a feather flock together"? Donors, customers, and volunteers can invite more quality people like themselves. That is, people who share similar philanthropic values. After all, you don't just want anyone to join your community. You seek one thousand fans just like your favorite volunteers, donors, and customers.

My husband is a Nature Conservancy Legacy Club member. As such, he receives select invitations for travel, field trips, and seminars. One of these recently included a field trip. As we considered attending an event, we decided to drive three hours to participate and to request four spots instead of two. Why? So we could invite another couple who we knew had an interest in the cause. That is, friends who'd be perfect for the Nature Conservancy.

Quicker Closes

We trust those our friends trust. People who arrive in your community by the recommendation of a donor, volunteer, or customer will like you faster. Our friends didn't need to have a relationship with the Nature Conservancy to attend their event. They attended based on our recommendation.

It also helps that when these newcomers get introduced to your organization, they often have already learned a great deal about your work from their contacts. They, therefore, ask 200-level questions, rather than 100-level questions. A referral asks, "How will you use my donation?" instead of, "Why do you need donations?"

In summary, by giving testimonials and inviting others, your donors, customers, and volunteers help you to reach your Magic Circle of Next *and* to close donations and sales more quickly. These newcomers will be much more likely than the general population to fit your picture of ideal supporters. This is why it's good for you. Why is it good for your donors, customers, and volunteers? Let's look at that now.

What's in It for Them?

Why would an opera donor bother to call a development staff member? How does it help your donors, customers, and volunteers? The answers are renewal, affirmation, leverage, and friends.

Renewal

Too many nonprofit leaders lose sleep at night fretting about donor burnout. Donor burnout occurs when contributors gets asked for funds repeatedly until that pool of contributors get exhausted.

Donors worry about burnout too. Individuals who love your cause want to see it succeed. They realize their limits, including that eventually they won't be around to give.

Burnout doesn't only happen with donors. It occurs with volunteers and, to some extent, customers. Volunteers see the work that needs doing. They seek to lighten their loads, to ensure that the work continues in their absence, and to take volunteering breaks, without detriment to your efforts.

How can you cure burnout? Grow your pool of supporters. What is the opposite of burnout? Reenergized people who enlist again. That is, donors who ask, "How can I help?" Volunteers who say, "I'm so glad to see the new volunteers joining us." Customers who mention, "I'm delighted you have enough people to provide another class option."

What reenergizes donors, volunteers, and customers?

- witnessing swelling of support for the cause
- a sense that they're riding a wave moving toward the vision
- the arrival of enthusiastic newcomers
- a recognition that success does not depend only on them

One benefit of engaging donors, volunteers, and customers in raising millions with you includes less burnout and more renewal.

Affirmation

Inviting people who subsequently connect to your favorite nonprofit is fun, empowering, and potentially life-enhancing, both for the newcomer and the recommender. It's affirming. Having someone you referred get connected supports your decision to get involved. Furthermore, it's heartening to give advice, see it used, *and* watch another person's condition improve.

Leverage

Challenge grants are a funding commitment to your nonprofit that requires the organization to obtain, by a deadline, a certain amount of dollars from other sources to match the original funds. You probably already know that challenge grants raise more money than requests without them.

Likewise, encouraging new people to get involved leverages the efforts of your existing donors and volunteers. For customers, a more substantial base of followers helps to assure that a popular service or product will continue.

Friends

In Dan Ariely's *Wall Street Journal* column, "Ask Ariely," he responded to a man asking how to create new friendships as a recent retiree. Ariely's advice was to pick an activity. He went on to say, "Don't worry if you don't like the activity very much: The other people are probably there for the same reason—to make friends." This proves true to those who refer others to your nonprofit—and imagine the impact when it really is something they enjoy.

Girl Scouts have sung "Make New Friends (But Keep the Old)" around campfires for more than fifty years. Customers, donors, and volunteers who refer existing friends and contacts create opportunities to keep old friends. Referrals to new acquaintances allow them to make new ones. Events at your nonprofit allows donors, customers, and volunteers to gather. Working with others to solve a difficult challenge deepens relationships more quickly than networking parties. Gathering at your organization helps a good cause, enhances existing friendships, and means people looking for new friends don't have to clean up their house for company.

Those are some of the reasons why your donors, volunteers, and customers benefit by helping you gather resources. Next we turn to how you might engage them in these tasks. To begin to answer that question, let's look at the Best Buddies model.

BEST PRACTICES

YES, THERE IS AN APP FOR THAT

Best Buddies is the world's largest organization dedicated to ending the social, physical, and economic isolation of the 200 million people with intellectual and developmental disabilities.

David Quilleon, the senior vice president for global mission, state development, and operations, shared with me that the organization's buddy-sponsor relationship drives enthusiasm, volunteer enlistment, staff dedication, and donor engagement. One significant way that Best Buddies shares connections is through stories. Like most nonprofits, Best Buddies uses stories to help fundraise, even if the tale-tellers and recipients don't know they're helping.

The Best Buddies Way

What was the best way for Best Buddies to collect stories? The organization's answer was to create an app that allows volunteers and staff to record interactions. Developing and using an app works for Best Buddies because their ultimate mission involves young people and executives interacting. Both populations are likely to use cell phones.

How is the app used in fundraising? Imagine you're sitting with a prospect, enjoying a networking lunch. You share with this new acquaintance a snippet about your organization. Your partner nods and looks around the room. When you open your phone and show them three buddy interactions happening in real time, they get enthusiastic. "Look. Right now a buddy's sharing lunch in Tucson. Here's a second in Denver, and another across town."

The stories the app captures generate support for fundraising and more. They also cement memories. What do I mean? Recall for a moment your high school experiences. Which do you remember? In all likelihood, they are the events for which you have photos, or a a video clip. Since the day you started high school, you lost zillions of different experiences, such as standing at your locker on the sixty-first day of freshman year. Posts in the Best Buddies app, like your high school pictures, reinforce experiences. What's more, the posts transform experiences into shareable memories.

How Can You Do That?

You probably collect mission stories. Do you do so in a way that engages your customers, donors, and volunteers in assembling them? How can you develop a system to gather mission moments? You might copy Best Buddies and develop an app. How else can you reap the benefits of collected stories? Here are several alternatives. Use them as a springboard to generate a story collection process for your nonprofit.

- Hand out selfie sticks at events and ask people to text you the pictures.
- Invite people to draw their experiences and create handmade art to reproduce and share.
- Collect video testimonials before, during, and after activities.
- Set up a photo booth with props that reflect your brand.
- Ask volunteers, donors, and customers to record a telephone message.

HOW TO CREATE VOLUNTEER, CUSTOMER, AND DONOR HEROES

Follow the Leader: Your Culture Models

When you adopt the Let's Raise Nonprofit Millions Together approach, your donors, customers, and volunteers will see examples of philanthropic power to change lives just by hanging around. This is good news. Who you are and what you do daily encourages people to join you and duplicate your efforts. When you model what you want others to do, you teach.

Modeling in and of itself influences. You can leave it at this and let the residue of modeling help you. Alternatively, you can establish a process where your donors, customers, and volunteers take steps to engage others.

First, let's look at a concern I'm sure you have. You wonder if it's okay to ask your donors, volunteers, and customers to do more. If you believe, as I advocate in this book, that when you offer people philanthropic opportunities, you provide life-changing value, you'll want to offer everyone the chance to invite others.

Working with donors, volunteers, and customers requires a gentle, low intensity, invitational approach. To proceed, I recommend you divide your donors, customers, and volunteers into two groups and approach each group differently.

Group One: Cheer, Support, and Coach Hand-Raisers

The first group comprises of those who raise their hands. Who are these people? Your donors, customers, and volunteers who call to tell you that they've invited friends.

What is the best response to their help? To cheer and thank the people who issue invitations. Also, as appropriate, to uplift their actions as exemplars to others. As the wisdom goes, if you want more of something, praise it.

After your mini-celebration, ask how you can support their efforts. For example, after a donor invites newcomers to your event, check back with them to learn how it went. Seek their advice. Inquire if there is anything you can do now or differently in the future. Ask if they need any collateral materials, such as brochures, videos, articles, or the like.

Besides cheering for the person and checking back with them, you might offer informal coaching to increase the odds of creating successful connections. Coaching here can include sharing what others learn and tips you personally find helpful. Just as you plan meetings to ask a donor for a major gift, assist willing donors, volunteers, and customers in developing a plan on how they will invite others.

Group Two: Listen and Be Accessible

Q: How can you work with donors, volunteers, and customers who don't raise their hands?

A: Carefully.

Occasionally, you'll encounter moments when you can encourage your supporters to invite others. Here's one scenario.

Your volunteer committee is meeting. The conversation turns to "them." Let's listen to fragments of the dialogue.

- "If only *they* would…"
- "*They* don't do enough…"
- "If *they* gave our budget would be…"

I call these conversations "if only *they* would do something" discussions. Do you hear the disappointment these words express? If you listen, you frequently hear these conversations whenever groups meet and resources are limited. The problem with these conversations? Blame never gathers: it repels. Those who get blamed don't care. Or if they do care, they've already been judged and they know it!

Most importantly, "if only *they*" conversations spiral downward, burn energy, and fail to empower the participants. In reality, the people who can change things sit at the table now. When we stop expecting others to do something and instead act, we create real change.

When you encounter "if only *they* would do something" conversations, discern if this dialogue is venting or an opportunity. Might the complaints represent a disguised request for help engaging others? If so, say, "Ah, you're talking about how to engage more people. Would you be interested in learning how we can engage more new folks?" Provide information, skills, and tools to change the current state of "not enough" and to create entrance ramps to your highway to a different future. Teach people how to successfully invite their friends and contacts to join you.

BRING IT HOME

REMEMBER HOW WE MET

When people express interest in helping others to join your organization, ask them to deconstruct how they got involved. Here's one option: Hand out paper and ask everyone to reconstruct a timeline of involvement in your nonprofit in detail. Ask everyone to share their story and listen for the common, repeatable patterns.

Besides occasions when people get wistful about engaging more people, when else will your donors, volunteers, and customers be open to growing their community and resource development skills? Here are several more circumstances:

- when they try to fill seats at an event
- at the start of a small or major campaign
- during volunteer and customer orientations
- when you introduce new tools and activities for newcomers
- when you offer outside expertise

Provide Doors

You read about how to support hand-raisers and others. Before closing this section, here's an essential ingredient to help your volunteers, donors, and customers gather others: options. That is, you'll want to provide many opportunities for newcomers to participate. Multiple, frequent, and fresh occasions act as entryways to your organization. Sharing different doors provides your volunteers, customers, and donors places to direct and drop off their contacts.

Here are some examples:

- open houses, such as when you open your new wing
- tours, such as museums, blood banks, and others,
- celebration experiences, such as Habitat for Humanity's Key Ceremonies and Citizen Schools' WOW! events
- guest speakers

Start by offering doorways quarterly. Over time, add monthly or even biweekly events to your calendar.

IMPORTANT

YOUR MOST IMPORTANT LONG-TERM RETURN ON INVESTMENT FROM THIS CHAPTER: BEQUESTS

Your most significant, most enthralling opportunity with donors, volunteers, and customers is bequests. Don't forget to invite these individuals to remember your nonprofit in their estate plans. Bequests average $70,000 and require an average of seven years to come to fruition. Therefore, bequests made today will not bear fruit for almost a decade. Don't you wish you had started asking people to remember you in their will a decade ago?

THREE TECHNIQUES TO HELP YOUR VOLUNTEERS, DONORS, AND CUSTOMERS EXTOL YOUR VIRTUES

So far in this chapter, you explored how your donors, volunteers, and customers can help you to grow resources, why it's in their best interest to do so, and some techniques to engage them. Let's explore three additional actions you can take to support your donors', volunteers', and customers' efforts to help you raise millions.

1. Keep Them Informed

People who don't know about your virtuous works are unlikely to support and recommend you to others. Therefore, create a process to share frequent updates with your donors, customers, and volunteers.

For instance, people who donate or buy products at Habitat for Humanity ReStores seek a place to unload their gently used items or capture bargains. Nonetheless, according to Barbara Inman Beck, president and CEO of Habitat for Humanity of Florida, Habitat affiliates do more than thank these customers for their purchase or contributions. Many stores have signs, information boards, brochures, and enlightening blurbs on receipts to inform the public about the homeowners and community benefits they are supporting. In a recent annual appeal, the Habitat affiliate in Highlands County, Florida, included people who made an in-kind donation to their stores. Of the new donations received, 45 percent came from ReStore donors.

2. Broadcast the Best Way to Help

Donors, volunteers, and customers already vote for your organization with their money and time. If they had a great experience, it's likely they're ready to refer you, give to you, or purchase from you again. To help them do so, share what would be most helpful. This is *not* asking for money—it's relaying facts. Inform people about what your organization needs to keep making mission. You do this with specific verbal and written phrases.

Here's an example of sharing what you need using words. For several summers now, I've attended Chautauqua Institution. It's a genial break from Florida's steamy heat. Besides its peak season summer in Western New York. The trees, the shrubs, and the foliage ache with the fullness of summer. Flowers line paths, fill triangle gardens, and jam front yards.

Last summer, I attended a presentation by Betsy Burgeson, supervisor of gardens and landscapes. You would love for your staff and volunteers to model Betsy. Here's why. Not only was her presentation informative, but at least twice, she deftly informed the audience about the best way to give. She explained that while funds for new gardens were welcome, "gifts that endowed gardens" helped the most.

Betsy told us that what was needed most were gifts that endowed gardens. What do you need exactly? Yes, money, but to do what?

Whatever you answer, convey your needs in a simple, memorable way. Betsy used the phrase "gifts that endowed gardens." What phrase can you use to help your supporters understand and remember what your nonprofit needs most?

Once you find these words, repeat them often. Weave them into your media. Broadcasting the best way to help supports your nonprofits to collect the resources it needs.

3. Request Testimonials Because It's Not Bragging When It's True

People listen to the advice of friends, neighbors, relatives, and people they know more than they listen to what you say about your organization. Donors, volunteers, and customers all have experience working with you. Capture their good words and use them.

I recommend you collect testimonials and use them in systematic ways to unleash their power. Your donors, volunteers, and customers love you and love what you do. What's keeping them from sharing their positive reviews of you? You never asked them.

Here are some tactics my clients use to collect reviews:

- When someone gives a compliment, ask if he or she would allow the organization to use that comment and their name.

- Do the same for comments received via email and text messages.

- Solicit live comments at events by standing ready to record videos.

- Ask for testimonials from your best customers, volunteers, and donors.

- Collect quotes and permission to use them as part of event evaluations.

By requesting testimonials, you'll gain words of wisdom to share with prospective donors, volunteers, and customers. Endorsements allow you to yell and shout about your good works without boasting. Learning about you from others will help you to grow your community, building your upward spiral of success.

In this chapter, you discovered how donors, volunteers, and customers can help you to grow your revenue and community. In the last few chapters, you have explored the role of boards and staff in raising millions together. I am thrilled to share the next chapter with you. Here, you will learn about who else can help you to raise millions together.

 ## YOUR NOT-TO-DO TIP

STOP PURUSING PEOPLE WHO DON'T RESPOND

Stop participating in "if only *they* would do something" discussions. *They* aren't coming. Instead, go out and invite new people. Help them to find you. Instead of complaining, use the time to grow your community.

CHAPTER TEN

SECRET TREASURES FROM UNUSUAL SOURCES: RAISING MILLIONS BY ENGAGING OTHER PARTNERS

About five years ago, Allegany Franciscan Ministries provided a grant to the local PBS affiliate, WEDU, and a regional healthcare collaborative to make a human trafficking documentary. When the ministry's staff discovered that the Junior League also shared an interest in ending human trafficking, they connected the three organizations. By joining forces, the groups drew over one thousand people to the film's first screening. It remains one of WEDU's most downloaded videos.

RAISING MILLIONS BY ENGAGING FOUNDATIONS, ASSOCIATIONS, ELECTED OFFICIALS, ADVISORS, AND OTHER PARTNERS

The Allegany Franciscan Ministries, a nonprofit that increases access to health care, is one of a small collection of "other entities" to enlist in your quest to raise millions. This chapter looks at individuals and entities, whom you may never have considered as partners, and how they can help you reach your goals. After reading it, you'll understand how every resource here can foster your revenue growth.

What makes this collection of people and institutions exceptionally interesting? First, they view the world from unique vantage points. These viewpoints allow them to see opportunities invisible to others. Second, since few nonprofit organizations recognize the full potential of these partners, you'll encounter slim competition. Finally, the others listed here will help you, if they can, because assisting you is in *their* interest. Each maintains a vested interest in your accomplishments.

Who are these others?

- foundations
- associations
- elected officials
- advisors
- partners who succeed when you succeed

With these sources, your path to obtaining resources will often require an indirect route. Moreover, as with all your efforts to secure revenue, income growth isn't guaranteed.

You will, however, gain support, respect, and fresh insights. These gains will help you achieve more, break through trouble spots, and discover new ways to grow your resources. As evidenced by what the stories ahead illustrate, their potential is astounding.

To get a better feel for what I'm talking about, let's return to look at the value that the Allegany Franciscan Ministries offered the three organizations it connected.

For WEDU, the health collaborative, and the Junior League, the connection provided:

1. a low-cost, high-return opportunity to join forces;
2. an expanded Magic Circle of Next;
3. the chance to demonstrate their ability to work with new entities midstream; and

4.   more impact on ending human trafficking.

For WEDU and the health collaborative, the referral offered:

1.   the potential to meet prospective board members and volunteers, because the Junior League's mission is to "develop the potential of women and improve communities through the effective action and leadership of trained volunteers."

For the Junior League, the recommendation delivered:

1.   an opportunity to partner with a widely recognized media outlet and to foster connections in the health field; and

2.   placement opportunities for their members that boosts the value of Junior League membership.

So far, this story lacks a million-dollar conclusion. Instead, it unveils the growth of a priceless resource pipeline. This chapter contains more stories *and* million-dollar opportunities. However, first, I'd like to introduce you to your other partners.

Drawing the Circle Bigger: A Who's Who Inventory of Overlooked Resources

Foundations and Other Funders

How Would You Respond to This Call?

The phone rang. Jill Vialet, the CEO and founder of Playworks, answered. Playworks is the leading national nonprofit leveraging the power of safe, fun, and healthy play at school every day; they're also known as "the recess people."

At the time, Playworks served schools in the Bay Area in California. The person calling explained that they were a staff member of the Robert Wood Johnson Foundation. "We've heard about your work in Oakland," the individual said, "and we would like to see an aggressive plan for Playworks to expand to serve the nation permanently."

Between the time Jill caught her breath and responded, she remembered several friends who liked to mess with her head. She said, "Who is this? *Really?*"

It *was* a staff member from the Robert Wood Johnson Foundation. Playworks subsequently received $4.4 million from the foundation to expand to three cities.

Besides grant funds, foundations and other funders provide resources and new connections for nonprofits. Why are these connections valuable to you? First, grant-giving entities read proposals for funding—often *lots* of them. While reading, they learn about trends, ideas, and leaders. Their review gives them a ten-thousand-foot view of what's going on in the nonprofit world. Say, for instance, a foundation announces an interest in literacy projects. You submit a proposal, along with twenty other entities. Subsequently, you receive a grant for 50 percent more than you requested, with the stipulation that you work with a new partner. This "more than you requested" funding is unusual but not impossible. I had the pleasure of hearing a client receive exactly this good news.

Not only do foundation staff members read proposals, but they also talk to civic leaders about needs. With this knowledge, they occasionally bring people together for the greater good. The Allegany Franciscan Ministries is one example of this kind of connection, and so is the unknown person who recommended Playworks to the Robert Wood Johnson Foundation.

Q: Why do foundations and other funders support your revenue growth efforts?

A: To leverage their investments.

Associations and Membership Groups

Continuing with our inventory of resources, let's look at groups whose mission is to serve nonprofits and specific industries. The first subgroup in this category includes associations, such as the Council of Family and Childcare Agencies, the Coalition for Behavioral Health, and your local arts alliance. A second subgroup contains state-wide, province-wide, national, or international organizations that charter, license, or permit you to represent yourself as an affiliate. Examples include Girls Inc., Meals on Wheels America, and Dress for Success.

Actively participating in association and membership groups increases your odds of growing income. First, you increase your chances of learning about and receiving government funding and pass-through grants. For example, with my consultation, Meals on Wheels PLUS of Manatee in Bradenton, Florida, received several grants from corporations by applying through Meals on Wheels of America.

Moreover, active associations and membership groups keep tabs on innovative activity among their membership. If you tap this knowledge, you can boost your resources. For instance, staff from these groups can point you to models to study practices you're considering. Building on what others learned saves time and money and, in some cases, allows you to tap their funding streams.

Knowledgeable staff act like tourist information centers in busy airports. They can direct you to resources, help you to compare alternatives, and give you an overview of options. In my years of tapping this resource, I've unearthed mixed results. Some staff members offer little; others share astounding insights. You never know what you'll find. Nonetheless, it pays to keep a channel on your radio tuned into associations and membership groups.

Q: Why do associations and membership groups support your revenue growth efforts?

A: To encourage membership growth.

 BEST PRACTICES

HARNESS THE PASSIONS OF YOUR CONSTITUENTS

Did you know that grassroots efforts have led to New York State providing more funding per capita for individuals with developmental disabilities than any state in the country? Tom McAlvanah, executive director of the InterAgency Council of Developmental Disabilities Agencies, shared with me how his agency's work helped the cause to reach this pinnacle.

His organization helps people to harness their passion and influence change. They help parents and individuals with disabilities to tell their stories. When parents say, "This is my son. He needs these services," legislators listen. One mother, for instance, informed officials that her ten-year-old son had eight teachers since the beginning of the school year—because of uncompetitive salaries. In turn, legislators share these compelling stories in committee meetings, which convince others to support change.

Here, for you to perfect, is Tom's formula to tap your grassroots energy to grow revenue:

1. Start with a firm understanding of your purpose.

2. Listen to your end users. Ask, "What do they want?"

3. Identify the common themes in their answers.

4. Seek funding for these shared needs.

5. As you seek funds, ask your end users to share their stories.

You can raise millions by directing the passions of your constituents to effective outlets, as modeled by the InterAgency Council of Developmental Disabilities Agencies. This is an association story, but it's also the story of another *other*, your legislative delegation. Let's turn to those we elect now.

Elected Officials

How can you work with your elected officials to raise millions? To answer this question, I talked to Ed Guthrie, CEO of Opportunity Village. Opportunity Village serves people with intellectual disabilities. Ed started with a story.

After ten years of invitations, the governor decided to visit Opportunity Village. On the appointed day, the CEO and chief development officer stood waiting at the door. When the governor arrived, Rosalie, one of the people Opportunity Village serves, preempted their plans. She rushed up to the governor and grabbed his hand.

"You must come," she implored, "and meet my friends."

When the governor departed thirty minutes later, he told Ed, "Rosalie has done more for Opportunity Village than all of you and your staff's visits combined."

Q: Why would elected officials support your revenue growth efforts?

A: To garner future votes.

BEST PRACTICES

GETTING THE GOVERNOR INTERESTED

When Ed Guthrie began his tenure as CEO twenty years ago, he and the board adopted a multiple-prong revenue strategy. One prong was to makes services for people with intellectual disabilities one of the top government funding priorities.

They decided to get influential people to tour the facilities and let the experience do the persuading. They included all elected officials, legislators, commissioners, governors, and officers from both sides of the aisle.

"I pick everyone," said Ed Guthrie, discussing his regular visits to Washington, DC, and Carson City.

How Can You Do That?

Call your elected officials. Meet with them. Ask them to experience your mission firsthand. Invite them to a performance, a Best Buddy lunch, to deliver a meal, or join with other volunteers on a workday. No matter their reply *this time*, establish a schedule to re-connect with your elected officials annually.

Expert Advisors

Our inventory of *other* continues with expert advisors. Unlike other groups in this chapter, you build this set of helpers. What I recommend is for you to develop a team of advisors to contact as needed. It's a bit like calling a friend in the television show *Who Wants to Be a Millionaire.* You connect with these advisors to see further, to tap the world's wisdom, and to be ready in case of contingencies.

You probably already have experts on tap. To expand this list, answer this question. If you could talk to experts in your field once or twice a year, who would you call? Use your answer to start your prospective expert advisor list.

Also, consider asking the following people to join your bench of advisors:

- consultants
- academic specialists
- top practitioners in the field
- for-profit business leaders whose markets overlap with yours
- any foundation president working on your challenge
- philanthropists
- former board members
- commercial real estate experts
- investment advisors
- human resources experts
- contractors
- board prospects

Creating a team of advisors allows you to engage people who live at a distance. You can also tap the wisdom of individuals who would never have the patience, time, or inclination to serve on a board or other task force.

By gaining access to their smarts, your advisors will help you to create a fabulously well-run organization that attracts notice and resources. You'll become a better leader by gaining insights, confirmation of your thinking, and fresh perspectives. You'll learn, for instance, the price of a property you're interested in purchasing—when you don't want your interest made public. You'll discover that a foundation is meeting to change their guidelines before you draft a proposal using the old ones. You'll learn that while offering continuing education credits seems like a revenue gold mine, it failed to work for a sister organization. Creating a stable of advisors allows you to funnel wisdom as needed into your organization.

Let's be clear. Some of these individuals will help you to raise revenue. Some, but not all, will require payment. Others will seek a quid pro quo arrangement. For example, one of my clients enlisted a university professor who expected, in return for his insights, to be able to invite the agency's customers to participate in his research. Your arrangements will depend on what you ask, their expertise, what they do for a living, and other factors.

Q: Why would advisors support your revenue growth efforts?

A: Your success will offer insights and forward movement in the sector in which they're deeply entrenched.

IMPORTANT

WORK-AROUNDS FOR BOARDS THAT WON'T FUNDRAISE

Nonprofit leaders spend an inordinate amount of effort trying to change boards that won't fundraise into boards that will. Recently, I worked with a sharp CEO with a "never board." The board had been hand-picked for compliance by a former CEO. Their recruitment came with the promise that they would never have to ask for money. They liked it that way.

If you find yourself tied to a board that "won't," develop an advisory team specifically to help you fundraise. Enlist advisors to gain an alternative source of wisdom and connections.

Partners, Friends, and Unknown Supporters

Last but not least in this inventory of other resources, let's look at the power of partnerships to bring resources to your table. Katrina Bellamere, with Parenting Matters, found that she increased her revenue and mission results by offering wraparound services for the families her organization serves. She provided these services by working with other nonprofits.

Funders and donors love nonprofit collaborative approaches. For them, it results in better services, reduced paperwork, and more chances to say *yes* to applicants. Katrina achieved her outcomes by seeking partners who were interested in the same results, shared credit, and were willing to work together so everyone's revenues grew.

Q: Why would other partners and friends support your revenue growth efforts?

A: They hold a vested interest in you or your work and hope that you'll return the favor someday.

Who else might you include as a potential resource? The answer depends on your mission and needs. As your Magic Circle of Next moves further and further into the community, you will discover more people who can help you to grow resources.

BEST PRACTICES

CREATE A THANK AND INFORM LIST

Foundations, associations, elected officials, advisors, and others, oh my! How can you take advantages of these development opportunities? Create a Thank and Inform List.

A Thank and Inform List is a record of the contacts you want to keep in touch with to help your organization. You use your list to organize your efforts. As a rule, once per quarter, you contact people on the list to update them about your needs and ideas and offer to help them. Your regular interaction keeps you at the top of these individuals' minds.

Small but Mighty

Seek a small group. You don't need everybody on your Thank and Inform List. You need a few stars to make your perfect constellation. To start, most clients focus their efforts on creating a team of ten or fewer individuals.

Prospects to Consider

Include people you already know. Add individuals you would like to meet and to whom you can introduce yourself, such as the CEO of a community foundation, elected officials, and leaders of special interest groups. Everyone you add should be someone with whom you believe your work will resonate and whom you respect.

Some people will self-identify. They'll stop you in networking meetings to give you advice. You'll get a call about what they see. To keep these gems flowing your way, include them on your list.

Besides people you know and admire, consider adding:

1. people who helped your organization but with whom you've lost contact;

2. individuals who significantly assisted your local nonprofit peers;

3. leaders in the community engaged in local interorganization leadership; and

4. people you like, respect, and with whom you share common ground.

As appropriate, move people on and off your list. For two years, you've wanted to meet the mayor. Finally, you do. In ten minutes, you discover the two of you lack connection. Like oil and vinegar, you both do great things, but you're not going to do them together. Take the mayor off the list.

Your Monthly Review and Quarterly Contacts

Use your Thank and Inform List to organize and remind yourself to keep information flowing to foundations, associations, elected officials, advisors, and other partners. Why do you need a reminder system with these folks? Because in most cases your paths only cross infrequently.

Here's the process I recommend:

1. Create a list. I've started an example one below.

Contact Name	Month One	Month Two	Month Three

Once per month, review the list. If you keep your list online, place a reminder in your calendar to check it.

2. During your review, note whom you've contacted. Jot the type of contact, such as "lunch," and a few words about the conversation's content.

3. Select the people you intend to contact next month. Determine how you will reach them. Your choices, from best to least useful, include: face-to-face meetings over a meal, face-to-face meetings elsewhere, a telephone call, a personal snail mail, an email, a text message, and, finally, crossing your fingers and hoping you'll see them at a networking event.

4. Either initiate a contact right away or note in your calendar when you will.

5. Put away your list until next month.

Help people on your Thank and Call List to be glad to hear from you. Make the goals of reaching out to renew the relationship, share updates, and express appreciation for the person's continued support. You can also ask how you might help your contact, and, as appropriate, ask them any other questions you have.

On average, each call will require a fifteen-minute investment four times a year. Your contacts, made in the spirit of mutual support, will provide an astounding hourly rate of return. You'll discover your organization:

- being mentioned as an example in presentations, interviews, or other public media in ways that helps you to grow your community;

- getting endorsed when a donor expresses interest in you;

- obtaining ideas, insights, and fresh perspectives; and

- receiving new revenue.

YOUR NOT-TO-DO TIP

NEVER MEET

Here's my big expert advisor tip: unless a project calls for it, never gather your advisors to meet. Instead, ask if they would be on-call for your questions. Reach out as you need, but don't make them attend another meeting.

CHAPTER ELEVEN

WHAT KEEPS YOU FROM RAISING MILLIONS? HOW TO BECOME A REVENUE HERO

Just a Fortunate Year?

As I made arrangements for a West Palm Beach, Florida, presentation, I asked everyone who was doing a great job in local development. The name I heard repeatedly was Vicki Pugh, who was the vice president of development at Palm Beach Atlantic University. The university had just finished its best fundraising year ever.

Vicki generously agreed to meet and share her analysis of what drove the university's success. These factors led Vicki and her team to the university's best funding year ever:

- The university's recognition that new revenue needed to come from generous donors since they faced tuition increase limits and space constraints.

- Vicki's work with faculty members to improve their resource development skills.

- Several bequests, though none substantial.

- The university president's development background and ongoing work with a coach planning donor engagements.

- Vicki and the president coordinating their efforts.

As I left Vicki's office, I was struck by the lack of miracles, secret spells, and large individual contributions in the triumph. Instead, I found dedicated staff with a clear purpose and disciplined efforts. The university knew what it needed to do and went about doing it.

That's how the resource development process works. You, too, can enjoy harvests like the one experienced by Palm Beach Atlantic University. Your results will come from using the process you learned in this book. Over time, you'll discover that some good development processes disappoint and other efforts, even weak ones, amaze. Mostly, you will, like Vicki, find that by consistently aligning your efforts, you produce exceptional results. Your outcomes will inspire and awe your colleagues and fill the local philanthropic community with buzz. Some of your peers will think you've developed a secret sauce. In truth, you trusted the process, worked it, and reaped the harvest.

On the other hand, in some ways, Vicki's year was lucky. How important was luck? I place luck fourth in this sequence:

1. the value you offer

2. the number of people to whom you offer the value

3. your ability to craft win-win-win opportunities for the nonprofit, the supporter, and the community, so people gain your value

4. luck

The university was lucky because enough donors decided to close their gifts in a single year so that the total the contributions broke all records. Vicki's success reflects the themes in this book, which are: focus on value, provide ongoing learning about income, build infrastructure into your culture, offer attractive choices, and embrace chaos. Before I share a self-management tool to help you create *your* best revenue year ever, let's review each theme and how it came to fruition at Palm Beach Atlantic University.

THEME ONE: FOCUS ON VALUE

Palm Beach Atlantic University determined how to provide amazing value to its donors and customers. You, too, offer fantastic value. Discovering your value and finding new value is critical to raising millions.

When Mark Haney was the vice president of advancement at the Florida Aquarium, he attended a Leadership Tampa Bay alumni event. Over drinks, he shared with friends that the aquarium was adding a children's deck, but unfortunately, they lacked the funds to put an awning over it.

A fellow Leadership Tampa Bay graduate, from TECO Energy, the local power company, asked if the cover might be designed to include solar panels. TECO was looking for public venues to install them. Mark said yes. Within two weeks, the aquarium obtained a $120,000 funding commitment.

This story about raising resources demonstrates that when others see your value and can paint themselves into your picture, they raise their hands to help. The TECO employee sought ways to benefit both TECO and the aquarium. To raise millions together, be value-driven.

THEME TWO: ONGOING INCOME EDUCATION

At Palm Beach Atlantic University, the president worked with a coach to plan donor engagements. Vicki worked with staff to direct their efforts toward individual donors and away from special events. As befits an educational institution, the university emphasizes education. When it comes to raising millions together, copy them.

Several years ago, I conducted an extensive research project on written works about fundraising and resource development. Once a week, I drove to a different library branch and brought home every book on fundraising. What I discovered were lots of texts on resource development that shared successful tactics. Topics included how to set up an office, send compelling emails, make calls, and other tasks.

I discovered scant information about why and how nonprofits convinced donors to donate. Most of the content reflected versions of this tale, "Once upon a time… and… then, we raised millions of dollars!" Your reaction is probably like mine. What happens between the start of the story and its happy ending.

This book works to fill in the ellipses, to explain how organizations translate a need for funds into receipt of them. I've dissected some of what is in customers' and donors' heads. To get to the happy ending at your organization, help people understand how fundraising and resource development works. You've read about the vital need for education throughout this book.

Having said that the information I found in my library research was mediocre, I still encourage you to dig in. Every book provided insight or an idea about better ways to work with boards, write annual appeals, and streamline efforts. Invest the ten thousand hours you need to become an expert. By reading, attending events, investing, and thinking about resource development, you'll learn even more ways to implement the Let's Raise Nonprofit Millions Together approach.

Don't just educate yourself-educate those around you. You get frustrated when your board doesn't get it. You get irritated with the staff's reluctance to help. You forget that gathering resources is not intuitive and that it conflicts with social norms about talking about money.

So ask yourself, what don't you get? How can you help others to get it more? How can you talk about your need for resources without feeling guilty, begging, or damaging relationships? You can answer all these questions and more with knowledge. Therefore, educate yourself and others.

THEME THREE: INFRASTRUCTURE CREATES CULTURE

Growing donations became part of the university's culture and infrastructure. Vicki and the president formed a fundraising team. The university supported Vicki's work with personnel to grow resources throughout the institution.

As you think about raising millions together, visualize your work as laying out a neighborhood complete with roads, playgrounds, ditches, lots, electrical grids, plumbing, and the like. You need these components to attract people to live in your community. Infrastructure, in the case of the nonprofit organization, involves all the processes and tools that link people to the cause and to each other. Your infrastructure includes development and marketing plans, the staff at the front desk, how you answer your phones, your standard for thanking donors, and more.

You want your infrastructure to support your viability, independence, and stability. So, build infrastructure to perpetuate your success. Construct it well, so that next year, raising each dollar takes less effort. Construct it so that everyone has a natural role in the resource development process. If you do so, in time, your infrastructure will both create and support a culture of philanthropy.

THEME FOUR: OFFER ATTRACTIVE CHOICES

Your value-driven, educated community helps you to seize opportunities and welcome individuals that cross your threshold. How can you take advantage of what newcomers bring? Offer interesting choices.

People like options. Although the approach in this book establishes a baseline that everybody helps, the approach includes individual choice. That is, everyone has a say in how he or she helps.

Just like parents who wisely ask their children to try new foods, encourage your supporters to test-drive new skills. Why? First, to learn. Second, they might love the experience, even if they heretofore found the thought distasteful. Third, after sampling the skills, they'll make informed choices.

The first time I was assigned to write a grant, I was partnering with a woman eight hours away. I had no interest in the effort but followed my boss's instructions. I was surprised to find I enjoyed the experience. I liked the possibility of new revenue, formulating an undeveloped idea, and the teamwork. Gradually, I learned to write high-value grants in hours. Eventually, as my skills developed, I wrote bulletproof requests that got funded and consistently outranked the competition. I wouldn't have done any of that if I wasn't assigned the first grant.

By offering thought-provoking options, you promote new skills, test plausible ideas, and insert innovation into your work. All these heighten the interest of people who raise funds with you and the community at large. Offering interesting choices results in increased job satisfaction and organization results.

Why does choice work so well? Because there are multiple paths to success. Choices take advantage of the assets you have today. Plus, you allow people to do what they love.

THEME FIVE: EMBRACE CHAOS

Implementing the Let's Raise Nonprofit Millions Together approach means that leaders are no longer the only people in a nonprofit who gather resources. Supporters help. By sharing power, you increase revenue, institutional learning, and resilience.

In the book *The Living Company*, Arie de Geus wrote about companies that lasted one hundred years and more. He writes, "Concentrated power means no freedom. No freedom means little knowledge creation and, worse, little knowledge propagation. No propagation means little institutional learning and, thus, no effective action if the world changes..."

Sharing power can also stir up chaos in busy nonprofits. How can you manage the turmoil? Pretend you are an air traffic controller at the world's busiest airport. Your job is to help the next plane to arrive safely. Once that craft lands, focus on the next jet, over and over again.

To deal with chaos, the last theme of this book, embrace one issue at a time. At the end of the day or before you start again, pause. Consider where changes can be made to improve your situation. Start those changes. Over time, with persistent effort, chaos will decline as you establish systems, habits, and better methods.

THE TRIFECTA OF MANAGEMENT

"You need to take care of yourself. You can't go to a board meeting feeling damaged. They'll eat you alive," advises Kristen Lessig-Schenerlein, client and former executive director of the Center of Anna Maria Island, who speaks from experience. She began her three-year tenure with an operating deficit plus capital debt and ended her service with both budgets in the black.

We've come to a critical pivot point in the Let's Raise Nonprofit Millions Together approach that I've brushed over until now. It is this: your leadership. As a leader of a nonprofit organization, you face a dual management challenge: the need to manage yourself and your supporters. So far in this book, you dove deep into leading others. Let's turn to self-management now, since your success also depends on you.

IMPORTANT

THE TRIFECTA OF SELF-MANAGEMENT

1. manage self

2. manage up

3. manage sideways and down

When I work with clients, at a certain point, their restlessness lets me know they've had enough. They're eager to stop talking and to fire up the ideas and put them into action. You're at that point and beyond. I've shared many ideas in this book. I have one last tool to share to inoculate you against two menaces you face: time management and the knowing-doing challenge.

OVERCOME THE KNOWING-DOING CHALLENGE

"Important things are put aside for the urgent until the important things become urgent and then sometimes it's too late." —Lee Boyan,

Successful Cold Call Selling

Rod, a nonprofit leader, attends workshops, reads avidly in the field, and discusses challenges with his peers. He thinks about how to improve the nonprofit he serves. He knows what to do to grow income. Nonetheless, it never gets done.

Rod faces the knowing-doing gap. Authors Jeffrey Pfeffer and Robert I. Sutton identified this behavior in their 1999 book *The Knowing-Doing Gap*. Humans suffer from this challenge in many facets of our lives. We often know what to do, but fail to do it—consider exercising regularly, not eating that dessert, and using praise instead of criticism to get better results from our others. You can master the knowing-doing challenge with better time management. Time management is a critical self-mastery tool for the Let's Raise Nonprofit Millions Together leader.

BEST PRACTICES

HELP! WE'VE GOT SO MUCH GOING ON THAT WE CAN'T GET TO THE STRATEGY!

In the office of Sharon Stapel, president of the Nonprofit New York, Sharon and I discussed the need for nonprofits to think, plan, and be strategic. We also considered the reality that many nonprofits live without the actual resources they need to meet their mission. Organizations want to be more strategic, but managing competing priorities leaves them little time. If this is your nonprofit, how might you move from your day-to-day busy-buzz to more strategic thinking?

Here's the plan:

1. Divide your board into two groups: Ask one group to address the current priorities. Ask the second team to design a sustainable strategy that would move beyond the constant urgency.

2. Invest one hour per month with your staff to imagine and prepare for a world with less frequent crises. Answer this question: "If we had time to plan and implement a strategy, what would that strategy be?"

3. With input from the staff and the board, dedicate one hour per month with your senior team to develop a strategy to deliver your organization to a place where crises become the exception. Design your roadmap. Include realistic components and sound actions that lead to specific results.

4. Start today.

Lucky Thirteen: The Ultimate Time Management Tool

This concept is adapted from the work of Alex Goldfayn, author of *The Revenue Growth Habit*, who formalized a process that I had less elegantly piecemealed together. The secret to the knowing-doing challenge is to break down tasks into small steps you complete early in the day. Find time to complete them by squelching less productive activities, such as checking social media. Researchers tell us that we spend one full workday a week tending to social media. The Lucky Thirteen tool takes advantage of this less-than-stellar time investment and assigns thirteen minutes a day to your top goal. To make progress on your most important goals, you can check your social media one less time per day, yes?

When it comes to Raising Nonprofit Millions Together, why do *you* especially need to commit to your top goal? Because the more you succeed, the larger your community of supporters. Your time constraints will increase. For instance, Jennifer Vigne, president of the Education Foundation of Sarasota County, shared with me a series of sixteen interactions that started when a business owner heard about the foundation's work on a public radio program. Over the next two years, the business, working with the foundation's staff, gave over $12,000 and lots of in-kind gifts.

Six Steps to Mastering the Lucky Thirteen

1. Identify Your Goal. What is the most critical area to make progress on this week? Draft a specific enough answer to this question that you can determine concrete actions that, when completed, show progress toward your priority. Increasing revenue, for instance, is too broad. Increasing donor revenue by 10 percent works. So does talking to your board members about connecting to a dozen business leaders.

2. *Identify Actions.* Brainstorm actions related to your goal to achieve in thirteen minutes or less. Your tasks don't need to take thirteen minutes or be completed in that time. You just need to make progress. For example:

- write a thank-you note to a donor
- call a board member
- set a regular weekly appointment with your development director
- create a staff meeting file with a reminder written in big letters to add an accountability process for every item
- make a prompt to keep board member prospects top of mind by pulling out a dedicated pad and listing your current candidates

3. Review Your Daily Routine. For each day, determine the thirteen minutes to invest. Make this your "instead of checking messages appointment" or ICMA. Select an appointment as early as possible when your willpower peaks.

4. Lock in on Your Target and Get to Work. Schedule your ICMA in your calendar. Commit to it. These few minutes are as important or more important to you than a call from your board chair, the local foundation, or the governor. Except under duress, don't ditch your appointment. Delay returning calls, checking emails, sending texts, or looking for information on the internet.

5. Make a Work Plan for the Following Week. Assign tasks from step two into your calendar for the five days. Once per week, plan your next actions. (You can count this task as your ICMA appointment for the day.)

6. Establish Accountability. Choose an accountability partner, ideally someone else using Lucky Thirteen. Once per week, share your successes by answering these questions in an email or text.

- How many days were you able to complete your thirteen minutes?
- What progress did you make?
- What will you achieve next week?

You can complete this in five minutes. Your email or text looks like this:

"Hi Kathy

1. Score: Five/five.
2. Done: Called or spoke to all my board members!
3. Next: Call five former board members.

You?"

Using Lucky Thirteen, you benefit from finishing small, practical, doable, and satisfying actions. Even in your busiest times, you make progress on your most important project. You put your top priorities on your desk daily and gain momentum, enhanced self-confidence, a greater sense of control, and hope.

RESULTS

Here are some client outcomes from Lucky Thirteen:

A: Stewarded donors. In sixty days, my client contacted every single donor on a donor list. The following year, donations increased by 45 percent.

B: Focused on corporate income. The CEO developed a list of twenty sponsors and doubled sponsorship revenue in six months.

C: Worked on obtaining new members. Membership grew by 10 percent after years of decline.

BEST PRACTICES

ALL HANDS ON DECK

The inspiration for this book came from a client experience with the Salvation Army of Sarasota, helping the staff to raise funds. Major Ethan Frizzell believes that all managers have a role to play in fundraising.

Over several months, I worked with the managers, holding small workshop sessions. Each session, we looked at the organization's income streams and explored how staff could help increase revenue. The process followed the themes in this book: offer value, learning, infrastructure growth, choice, and comfort with chaos.

When the staff wandered into the first meeting, reluctance dripped from the walls. They made small talk with each other, glanced at their watches and phones, and interacted stiffly with me. I asked them why they were passionate about their work.

Fast forward six months. At the closeout meeting with leadership, I learned that the managers--the same managers from five months earlier--were in another meeting room in the complex. "You won't believe it," the development director told me. "They were bragging about what they had done and how they helped develop resources. They were telling members of another corp that they should help raise resources too."

The Let's Raise Nonprofit Millions Together approach works. How will you use it to work for you?

THIS IS NOT A DEATH MARCH

Please don't take the Let's Raise Nonprofit Millions Together approach overly seriously. Have fun. Play. Employ a joyful spirit as you work. Seek to delight your donors and customers. You're on an adventure, and you don't have to sleep in the woods, use the outhouse, or get mosquito bites. Nonetheless, you still get to see a beautiful sunrise over your organization.

When you make plans, ask yourself: "Did I include fun?" If not, go back and add it. People want to enjoy being part of your community.

Need other not-to-do items?

Check out *kedconsultt.com/LetsRaiseMillions* for more not-to-do tips. To access the bonus materials, use the code: together.

APPENDIX A

TOOLS YOU CAN USE

Karen's Friends and Fortune Flowchart
Baseline Measurement

Rank how well members of your current community use each of the six skills. Use a one-to-ten scale, with ten equaling the high score. You can also download a copy of this chart at *kedconsult.com/LetsRaiseMillions*, password: together

For example, consider your board. Do your members act as hosts when they gather for meetings? How about if they stop by your office and spot someone in the lobby? Same question for special events. If they never host, give them a one. If they host in some settings but not all, it's a five. If they consistently greet newcomers and initiate conversations, award them a ten. If you have folks all over the continuum, call it a five. Continue by evaluating your staff, volunteers, and donors.

Skill	Board	Staff	Volunteers	Donors
Hosts				
Speaks				
Solves				
Invites				
Collects				
Introduces				

APPENDIX B

GLOSSARY

Bequest: A type of planned giving where an individual gives a gift to a nonprofit from their estate.

Case: A case is the reasons, often written, your nonprofit needs funds and how having them will change or improve lives. Strong cases include emotional and logical information about the need for and the benefits of your work.

Challenge grant: A challenge grant is a funding commitment to your nonprofit that requires you to raise, by a deadline, a certain amount of funds from other sources. If you raise the additional funds, the funder awards you the challenge grant.

Community foundation: Community foundations serve a specific group of people, such as the residents of Toronto or a subpopulation, such as Lutherans. Community foundations collect funds from a variety of donors, earn management fees on the funds, and oversee grant awards to nonprofits based on the goals of the donors and foundation.

Corporate income: Corporate income is nonprofit income from a business, corporation, or for-profit entitys often taking the form of event sponsorships, advertisement purchases, or grants.

Culture of philanthropy: A culture of philanthropy is a set of shared operating values around the role of individual donations in a nonprofit. These values include that everyone has a role to play in obtaining and contributing at the highest level possible. In a culture of philanthropy, the board, staff, volunteers, customers, and others live out these values.

Development: The process nonprofits use to help people to grow philanthropically. Colleges and universities often called this process advancement.

Donor burnout: You have donor burnout when too few contributors get asked for funds over and over again and they get tuckered out.

Government funding: You earn government funding by providing services—usually for community good—paid for with tax dollars. This funding usually requires extensive paperwork.

Grant: A grant is money given to a nonprofit to complete a specific activity or project.

Fundraising: The process of educating your prospect about the value of your work to improve their lives and others lives, and to raise donated income.

Giving circle: A giving circle is a type of philanthropy where individuals join together, contribute to a pool of money, and decide as a group which charities or community projects they will support.

Individual donations: Gifts from individuals and families to benefit your mission.

In-kind gifts/donations: In-kind gifts or donations are contributions of goods and services that nonprofits receive free or at low cost.

Karen's Friends and Fortune Flowchart: A set of behaviors that supporters of nonprofits can practice to grow revenue and the community, and to further a nonprofit's mission.

Learned optimism: Learned optimism is the idea that a talent for joy, like any other emotions, can be cultivated. The concept comes out of positive psychology and the work of Martin Seligman. He has a book of the same name.

Magic Circle of Next: A Magic Circle of Next is a group of people you don't know yet. You do, however, know someone who knows them.

Major gift: A major gift is an individual donation of such magnitude that it excites everyone at your nonprofit. Each nonprofit determines its own definition of what constitutes a major gift.

Mission: Your mission is the human or societal situation your organization addresses.

Mission income: Mission income is funding your nonprofit earns by doing its mission and providing services or products associated with it.

Other income: Other income is revenue that your nonprofit earns from providing a service or from selling goods when the product or service has little or no relationship to your mission.

Overhead: Expenditures you make to cover the costs of operating your nonprofit are overhead. Traditionally, you exclude expenses related to delivering programs and doing your mission from overhead calculations.

Passion: A sincere personal motive to care about a cause at the center of your work.

Philanthropy: The act of using personal resources to help others.

Planned gift: Planned gifts are donations that will be given in the future. Bequests are the majority of planned gifts. Planned gifts often include assets such as shares of stock or a piece of property. The donor's advisor—such as a CPA, lawyer, or financial planner—often participates in the decision and execution process.

Prospect research: Prospect research is the process of gathering public information about individual donors to learn their potential for making a major gift and that gift's potential size.

Special event: A special event is an event designed to raise money, increase relationships with current donors, and, ideally, create new friends.

Sponsorship: A sponsorship can involve a nonprofit receiving cash support from a business or other entity in exchange for recognition at a special event. Sponsorships also include much more. Well-developed sponsorships contain packages that include advertising, cause marketing, events, and ways to experience the business's service or product. Businesses partner with nonprofits to obtain branding, employee support, and to improve the community in which they operate.

Stewardship: In the nonprofit setting, stewardship is the act of caring for donors. This caring includes sharing your gratitude, expressing how the gifts helped, and telling how else the donor might engage in your nonprofit's work.

Strategy: A strategy is a course of actions to reach a goal. It tells, given your conditions, how you plan to win. Strategies outline the high level, big picture concepts you plan to use to take advantage of your skills and gifts and overcome your challenges.

Value: Value is the usefulness, importance, or worth or something to others.

APPENDIX C

ADDITIONAL RESOURCES

Dan Ariely: Ariely researches behavioral economics and writes about it in plain language. Ariely is the James B. Duke Professor of Psychology and Behavioral Economics at Duke University and is the founder of the Center for Advanced Hindsight. His work is important to the nonprofit professional because of the clarity it provides on ethics and the dishonesty we all practice. He is the author of several books.

The Association of Fundraising Professionals (AFP): AFP is a "professional association of individuals and organizations that generate philanthropic support for a wide variety of charitable institutions." Chapters meet throughout North America. See *afpnet.org.*

BoardSource: BoardSource is a national organization "for funders, partners, and nonprofit leaders who want to magnify their impact within their community through exceptional governance practices." BoardSource is a useful resource for sample policies, such as the gift-acceptance policy. See *boardsource.org.*

Canada Revenue Agency: The Canada Revenue Agency maintains a website where you can learn more about Canadian charities. Here you can view a charity's registered charity information return. See *cra-arc.gc.ca/charities.*

Candid: Candid is a new organization formed by the merger of the Foundation Center and GuideStar. Historically, the Foundation Center operated a useful website for learning about foundations in the United States and their funding patterns. GuideStar's website was helpful to learn about specific nonprofits.

Charity Navigator: As of this writing, Charity Navigator is the largest evaluator of charities in the United States. Some of your donors will review this site to learn more about your nonprofit before giving. The site offers information on its evaluation methodology used to help determine if your nonprofit meets or exceeds standards. See *charitynavigator.org.*

Community Foundation Locator: The Council on Foundations provides a map to help you identify community foundations that serve your area. See *cof.org/community-foundation-locator.*

Independent Sector: Independent Sector publishes a yearly report on the value of a volunteer hour of labor. Search for Value of Volunteer Time at *independentsector.org*

Karen Eber Davis Consulting: Karen's website contains over one hundred free articles, podcasts, and videos as well as access to her newsletter, *Added Value.* Updates to this book will be posted on this site as well. Visit *kedconsult.com/LetsRaiseMillions* Password: together.

The Partnership for Philanthropic Planning: This group promotes research, best practices, education, and gift-planning standards. Over one hundred affiliated local organizations hold regular meetings where you can learn more about planned giving and meet professional advisors. Go to *pppnet.org*

7 Nonprofit Income Streams: Both the number of nonprofit revenue streams and the title of Karen's book. Download a free chapter here: *kedconsult.com/download-free-chapter.*

Timetastic: Time Management for Nonprofit Leaders: Karen's time management tips booklet. Available from Amazon.

Interested in working with Karen? She looks forward to it. Please visit *kedconsult.com* to learn more about Karen's consulting practice, speaking, and mentoring program.

INDEX

A

B

C

corporate funding   39, 41

culture of philanthropy   2, 3, 6, 7, 37, 42, 113, 136, 139, 207, 218

customers   6, 13, 15, 16, 37, 42, 48, 49, 52, 59, 65, 72, 80, 83, 92, 95, 99, 117, 134, 137, 169, 170, 171, 172, 173, 174, 175, 176, 177, 178, 179, 181, 182, 183, 184, 185, 196, 205, 206, 216, 218

D

development director   7, 55, 65, 154, 155, 157, 162, 169, 170, 213, 215

development staff   2, 7, 12, 13, 37, 53, 59, 67, 137, 149, 151, 152, 153, 154, 156, 160, 162, 165, 166, 167, 173

donations   9, 21, 84, 109, 137, 153, 173, 183, 207, 214, 218, 219, 220

donor magic   137

E

Eckerd College   13, 131, 146, 163

elected officials   6, 48, 187, 188, 193, 194, 198, 199

endowment   45, 50

estate plans   182

expert advisors   194

F

fear of fundraising   83

Florida Orchestra   97, 145, 146

foundations   6, 12, 20, 39, 48, 125, 187, 188, 189, 190, 198, 199, 218, 222, 223

Friends and Fortune Flowchart   50, 51, 61, 64, 66, 68, 70, 72, 83, 124, 139, 143, 217, 219

funding streams   118, 191

fundraising fundamentals   41

G

generosity   78, 79, 85, 86

Girls Inc.   69

CPSIA information can be obtained
at www.ICGtesting.com
Printed in the USA
LVHW040324151019
634227LV00021B/2342/P